Publications of the Academy of American Franciscan History

MONOGRAPH SERIES, VOLUME THREE

Painting and Sculpture at
Mission Santa Barbara

Painting and Sculpture at
Mission Santa Barbara

Fray Junipero Serra, O.F.M., *Apostle of California*

PAINTING AND SCULPTURE

AT

MISSION SANTA BARBARA

KURT BAER

MCMLV

ACADEMY OF AMERICAN FRANCISCAN HISTORY

WASHINGTON, D.C.

Nihil obstat: BEDE A. DAUPHINEE, O.F.M., *Censor deputatus*
Imprimatur: † PATRICK A. O'BOYLE, *Archbishop of Washington*
August 9, 1955

To the memory of

PADRE JUNIPERO SERRA

who brought the first art to

California

Foreword

Junípero Serra, a retired university professor, led the pioneer Spanish Padres to California. Fray Francisco Palóu left his professor's chair in Mallorca to write the history of the frontier Missions as an eyewitness. University professors ever since have valued their work and evaluated their achievements.

The University of California has a brilliant record of research into the Spanish colonial period of our Southwest. Drs. Bolton, Priestley and Chapman refined the rich deposits of the Bancroft Library and added their own finds in Mexico, Spain, and elsewhere.

The source books they produced are used by writers of today who wish to view the entire picture under different lights or to add local color by their own knowledge of particulars. Thus the specialized formulas of dietetics have been used by Dr. S. F. Cook to estimate the impact of white civilization on the Indian's body. Now Dr. Kurt Baer has studied what sort of food for mind and heart was brought the California Indian by the Padres.

This is an inventory of a house where God and man have lived together peacefully a good long time. Some of its furnishings are commonplace, some are beautiful, some few exquisite. In Spanish days probably no one found every sacred image here inspiring or even pleasing. Tastes differed then as now. There is little record of what artistic reaction this statue or that picture produced.

We know these are the things that helped other people to be good by giving them some visible expression of their faith, some tangible reminder of their brethren in Christ, the saints. Now, to learn what land and hand produced these images, and just how and when they came to be assembled here, helps us appreciate this Mission's place in the slow interweaving of different centuries and cultures.

With patient scholarship and good taste, Dr. Baer has deepened and defined our appreciation of California's past.

ERIC O'BRIEN, O.F.M.

Mission Santa Barbara, California

Contents

Illustrations

Illustrations *(continued)*

Illustrations *(continued)*

Illustrations *(continued)*

Preface

This work is intended as a guide to and study of the paintings and sculpture of Mission Santa Barbara. Because of the nature of the Mission as a church, a seminary, and a residence for the clergy, much of the material herein listed and described may not be seen by the layman. It has, however, been included in the general catalogue because of its historical as well as its artistic association and interest. The question of the artistic merit of any piece has not entered into the consideration of inclusion; good or bad, they are all a part of the collection.

In such a work as this, where documentary evidence as to the exact origin of the sculpture and painting is virtually lacking, much must of necessity depend upon comparative study and assumption. The regrettable absence of signatures on the majority of the paintings can to some extent be attributed to the practice of concealing what might be works of important masters; that is, the signed work by a ranking artist might (as was often the case) disappear from so public a building as a church. Also, many were painted by priests and friars trained in the arts; their work was almost never signed. On the other hand, many paintings and sculptures were the products of studios of leading artists and academies in Mexico City and other centers; they in a sense mass-produced the works for the hundreds of churches and missions in Spanish Colonial America, especially during the eighteenth century. In any event, much of the early history of these works is no longer known. Every available book describing the Mission, or which might have mentioned some or any of the works contained in it, and which has been written during the past 150 years, has been carefully read with the hope of finding possible clues as to the origin, the identity of the artist, or the school of the work in question. In general, the attributing of many paintings to celebrated artists made by writers in the past has been grossly inaccurate in almost every instance.

As a consequence this volume is a catalogue of works first and a classification second. Future examination of archival material, it is hoped, will make it possible to assign properly much of the material now seriously in question.

It is due to the co-operation of the clergy at Mission Santa Barbara that I am indebted first for permission to produce this comprehensive catalogue, something which has not previously been attempted as a part of California Mission history, and secondly, for their assistance in many matters. To Father David Temple, O.F.M., Provincial; to Fathers Fabian Gussenhoven, O.F.M., and Basil Kelly, O.F.M., the former and present guardians of the Mission, for their patient counsel and encouragement over a period of considerable time; to Father Maynard Geiger, O.F.M., historian of St. Barbara Province, who made accessible to me many old documents and photographs, I am above all grateful. To Brothers Michael, Leonard, and Mark, whose interest and general enthusiasm in many ways made the task a genuine pleasure, I also give thanks.

The difficulty of photographing many of the faded and damaged works was eased considerably by the assistance of Fathers Kiernan and Emory of the Old Mission, and by Ray Borges and Robert McCoy, who made many of the pictures in the catalogue. My sincere appreciation for assistance in proofreading and suggestions goes to Patricia Dayton and Diana Ayres Cary, and to Dorothy Bridgehouse for preparing the final manuscript. Mrs. Violet Shue of the Santa Barbara College Library has been of inestimable help in locating and procuring scarce books and documents for comparative study.

Acknowledgement is due the University of California Press, the Museum of Modern Art, N. Y., the Bancroft Library of the University of California, The Book Club of California, Little, Brown, and Company, and the Historical Society of Southern California, for permission to quote passages from their publications and to use photographs in their possession.

Santa Barbara, California   K.B.

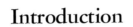

Introduction

Introduction

Throughout the world the churches of Christendom, and especially the Catholic churches, have been erected and have been beautified for the greater honor and glory of God. It is no wonder that the churches the length and breadth of Europe are for the most part superbly and magnificently decorated. There, for centuries, from the fall of the Roman Empire to the present day, the Church had at its disposal the greatest names in the fields of the arts. Not only was ecclesiastical ornament developed with increasing magnificence and variety as the Church spread, but the taste and the efforts of its millions of worshipers grew apace with it. When a new altar, or a new painting, or a new sculpture was blessed, it was expected to be more or less in accordance with traditional as well as contemporary forms of expression and was invariably accepted, and usually the occasion of celebration.

But the decoration and even the very construction of the missions of California and of Texas, New Mexico, and Arizona were no small wonder. The incredible faith and confidence of a mere handful of Jesuit and Franciscan padres, removed from civilized centers by literally thousands of miles of deserts, mountains, and seas, and in the midst of relatively unintelligent, semi-primitive pagan Indians, the faith that produced an architecture and accumulated a wealth of painting and sculpture as well as other decoration, that faith and its results was indeed for the greater glory of God.

In California, the Apostolic Father Junípero Serra had participated materially not only in the founding but in the building of the missions, especially in the first constructons at Monterey and Carmel, though indeed the style and the method of those early primitive buildings were in no sense as elaborate as the buildings one sees today. While none of the great stone churches was built during his lifetime, the ruins of the adobe buildings of the earliest period are convincing proofs of his skill as a builder. These crude buildings were at least in the spirit of the primitive modesty "prescribed by our Father, St. Francis." Within that modesty they were constantly improved without interruption; they grew with the richness and success that surrounded them. Out of this development came the "mission style," and the missions rank in importance architecturally with the historic buildings of the colonial period of the Atlantic coast.

There are architects who deny the existence of such a style and who question the originality of Franciscan architecture, especially in California. For them, it is but an eclectic composite of far superior Spanish urban styles, which, having descended to the outposts of California, found expression in crudeness of materials, in simplicity of forms, and because of their functional needs, the characteristic pattern.

Fig. 1.   THE CHURCH OF TANCOYAL,
SIERRA GORDA, MEXICO

The style, however, is genuinely the product of its surroundings; it is distinctly and characteristically indigenous. It had been difficult if not impossible for artists and artisans to come to California at that early period, and it was rather the priests and the Indians for the most part, who, using materials at hand, meeting and solving the problems as they arose, unwittingly created that distinctive style.

William L. Judson wrote and believed in 1905 that "these plans [for the missions] were brought ready made from Spain or Mexico" rather than that "the priests themselves were trained architects," for the "maturity of design, the richness of elaboration in the plan, and the adaptation of parts to each other . . . seem convincing evidence that master minds and experienced hands first conceived and drew the plans. There is no record of skilled artists."[1] Such commentators overlook the fact that a considerable number of the priests worked as missionaries under not too dissimilar conditions in the Sierra Gorda district north of Mexico City, and this gave them considerable experience. Serra himself supervised the building of five churches, all the more remarkable because of their very elaborate style in that isolated mountain area. Some of the padres were in the Sierra for nearly twenty years; Paterna and Crespí, as well as Lasuén and Palóu worked and served there. They were all experienced men; each mission church that they built was individually suited to the needs at hand. Furthermore, not only were they religious men whose central interest was spreading the Faith, but they were scholars of the first rank before they became missionaries. They had at their disposal the books and libraries not only of the Church but of the State; they had the knowledge that grew out of the experience in the founding of the missions throughout New Spain. The very fact of the great variety in plan of the missions, their very individualism, precludes the assumption that

Fig. 2. THE "MIRACLE" AT SAN GABRIEL

other minds drew up the plans. When the padres came to California they brought with them not only an apostolic but a practical training. That artisans, masons, and engineers were brought to California is true, but that did not occur until the last years of the eighteenth century. Bancroft lists a surprising number of carpenters, mechanics, and smiths, most of them arriving between 1792 and 1795.[2] One is mentioned by name, Alberto Córdoba.

The form and style of the early California buildings grew logically out of the functional demands of the moment; what ornamental embellishments exist were a blending of remembered or copied orders and devices of architectural style that because of the almost primitive construction methods became integral rather than superficial parts of the mission churches in particular. Furthermore, it is evident that the man who built the missions loved architecture for its own sake, for no one was there to admire it save the Indians. (See Figure 1.) These churches were not only expressions of faith but also a means through which the padres retained their hold on the highest conventions of civilization. Father Serra did not, intentionally or no, bequeath to posterity a finished, masterly architecture, but rather an architectural movement that has continually retained its influence to the present.

It is also true that in the beginning of the missions in California there were no masterpieces by Raphaels, Lippis, or Murillos. It is true that the finest art procurable was obviously not to be sent to such then remote outposts as San Gabriel or Santa Barbara, whose continued existence often was doubtful. However, it is to the credit of none other than Father Serra that paintings and sculpture of "good quality" were brought to these early outposts. Perhaps some of the works were never, even at their sources, considered worth very much. Artistically, and from a purely critical point of view, a majority of existing paintings in the California and other missions may leave a great deal to be desired. Yet the fact remains that in these missions, as in those of Arizona and New Mexico, are the oldest collections of seventeenth- and eighteenth-century art, and particularly religious art, in this country. It is quite probable that many paintings and sculptures had come directly from Spain. The Spanish Franciscan historian Juan de Torquemada, O.F.M. (1550-1625),[3] and Bernal Díaz, and the Franciscan Toribio Benavente (better known as Motolinía), among others, all record the transporting of many pieces of religious sculpture and painting from Europe. This took place with the coming of the first missionaries to Mexico. Because of the fact that in the sixteenth century the Netherlands were under Spanish rule, much Flemish art was in-

Fig. 3.   OUR LADY OF SORROWS

troduced into Spain, and consequently influenced the native art; it is therefore frequently possible to date a mission painting approximately from its technique and style up to about the latter third of the sixteenth century, for the style was Flemish rather than Spanish, especially in Mexico. There are many examples of Flemish tapestries, paintings, and sculpture in Mexico; they had been brought directly to the New World from Spanish convents and monasteries, or through the bequests of wealthy patrons of the Church.

Although no important Flemish paintings have been discovered in the missions, engravings probably originating in Flanders are in several collections. A prodigious number of engravings was made to illustrate missals and other religious books; these originated in the presses of the Flemings, who often removed their establishments to Spain during the seventeenth century. Engravings were the main means for the dissemination of "paintings," and not infrequently the original underwent some modifications. In later years the subject matter varied considerably, so that much secular material also appeared for distribution. The engravings themselves were originally derived from accredited and accepted—and in some instances, popular—works in the churches and "collections" in Spain and Flanders and, occasionally, in Italy. The practice of copying these engravings, or their use as models by minor painters, endured well into the latter years of the eighteenth century in Mexico. At Santa Ines Mission, the model for the Tenth Station of the Cross is a Venetian engraving dated 1778.

The majority of the existing works were made in and around Mexico City, and around Zacatecas, Puebla, San Miguel de Allende, before Mexico's independence from Spain in 1821; many of the painters were Italians and Spaniards who had come as early as the sixteenth century to the New World to establish themselves. The European supply of decorative material for Mexican, and subsequently Californian—to say nothing of South American—churches soon could no longer keep up with the demand. The need early arose for art production in the new countries; this brought about the rise of native schools and native artists, which resulted in the first period of Mexican colonial art, dating from shortly after 1521. One characteristic of the architecture of this period was the *mudéjar* style, which was Spanish (or Christian) work created in the manner of the late Moorish so prevalent in Spain, and brought to the New World. It can be seen in the carved wooden ceilings and other decorations of many churches throughout Spanish Colonial America. Both the "Moorish" architecture and the designs on ceilings are to be found in Santa Barbara.

One of the earliest academies, under the patronage of the Viceroy Mendoza, was that at Santiago Tlaltelolco, attached to the Franciscan monastery in the Indian quarter of Mexico City. There the Aztec Indians were taught, in addition to music, the techniques of carving, painting, and decorating the various accessories for use in churches. For their models they had the imported works from Flanders and Spain. Thus, the influence on Mexican art, and painting in particular, was Flemish, Italian, and Spanish. The first and one of the most important leaders in teaching the Indians painting and sculpture was Fray Pedro de Gante.[4] By 1535, sixteen years after the entry of Cortez into the city of Mexico, Spanish art was already firmly established. Through the importation of finer models the native workers were becoming skilled copyists. Not only easel paintings, but frescoes were attempted, and lacking examples of fresco work in the early period, the Indians copied woodcuts or engravings from religious books. The resultant work was not only linear in character but essentially black and white. The presence of Spanish art and artists was a stimulus to the development of native Mexican talent, but by the end of the sixteenth century copying had to a large extent disappeared, and the Indians were doing creative work. This was the second period of Mexican colonial art; it was influenced by the Spanish Renaissance and lasted almost to the middle of the seventeenth century.

Spanish sculpture during the first hundred years of Spanish rule in the Americas was almost wholly Andalusian in character; it included everything from enormous and elaborate reredos to very small figures. The carving of devotional sculpture was the chief task of the seventeenth-century sculptor in Spain. The majority of such pieces were colored to imitate life. As a national art this painted sculpture had scarcely been known beyond its boundaries, but it is well deserving of notice for the remarkable effects it sometimes displayed. The use of color in Spanish statuary was of considerable antiquity, "whether considered as a relic of classical times or as a practice encouraged or introduced by the Church to aid the illusion with which she strove to invest her worship and move the spirits of the faithful."[5]

The Immaculate Conception (the *Inmaculada*), a most frequent representation of the Virgin in both Mexican and Spanish art, first appeared early in the sixteenth century in Spain. It rapidly became

Fig. 4. THE "CLOCK" MISSION

the accepted and symbolic type. The Virgin stands on the crescent moon, sometimes also on the serpent (of evil); her body is somewhat turned in a twisting upward movement, with the left hand resting on her breast and the right holding a lily. The face may or may not be turned upward. One of the first examples of the type was Juan de Juni's central figure of the altarpiece in the Church of Santa María in Medina de Ríoseco near Valladolid, dated 1565. Already a postured mannerism is evidenced. This rather abnormal pose was significant of the meaning, and the forms used by him and later artists, both painters and sculptors, became expressive symbols of ecstatic abandonment.

Fig. 5. THE MISSION IN 1850 (from a drawing by H.M.T. Powell)

Yet another very popular presentation was the Mother of Sorrows, the *Mater Dolorosa,* either alone or present at the Crucifixion. The early works (sixteenth century) representing the *Dolorosa* show her usually without the sword in her breast, or without the rays. Because of the intense piety and devotional realism of the period, the artist was very eager to give what to him was a truthful rendering of the tragic theme. The result of this tendency was an uncompromisingly "realistic" portrayal, with considerable facial distortion that had no regard for traditional (i.e., Italian) physical beauty. Another type of the Sorrowful Mother was the *Pietà,* which, though it took many forms, eventually became a stereotype. Juni in 1571 created a large, complex group for the Cathedral at Segovia that was a curious mixture of affectation and striving for effective realism. Traces of the influence of Michelangelo are in evidence; however, the essential character of the scene with its theatricalism was generally all that was copied or adapted when the style reached Mexico a short time later.[6]

The unfortunate decline of Spanish, and with it Mexican, sculpture into a state of banality is clear in the work of the Spaniard Gregorio Hernández of Castile, who strove for deliberate naturalism. In contrast to the earlier polychromy of sculpture, much of it with gold predominating, the coloring or painting of wooden figures for a greater illusion of reality was undertaken. With this tendency developed the custom of using other than sculptural materials. Eyes were made of glass or porcelain and set into sockets rimmed with real lashes; genuine hair was affixed, and glass or crystal beads were set into the cheeks to suggest glistening tears. There are several examples of this type of work in the California Missions. In the Passion, and especially in the Crucifixion, the physical distortion and disfiguring of Christ was a common practice. The large Crucifix on the Santa Barbara Reredos has the flesh of the corpus torn to the extent that the ribs in the back show. These were displayed to harrow the feelings and to arouse the religious compassion of the beholder.

In order that they be as lifelike as possible, and the better to strike the imagination, most statues in Spanish churches and convents were actually clothed in the proper garments; St. Bernard of Clairvaux, for example, was habited in the robes of the Order. The practice is still common in Mexican and in some California churches, especially on feast days.

Examples of statues with movable arms, hands, and heads can be found in many Spanish and Mexican churches. Originally these figures were intended to be carried on carts in processions; the comparison with the stage, the *autos sacramentales,* is very clear.

On the other hand, the dignity of the classical was not wholly absent in Spanish sculpture. Perhaps the greatest of the masters was Martínez Montañés (1568-1649), whose combining of realism with the classical was a considerable influence on at least one phase of the art. The Crucified Christ is a common subject in Spanish Baroque sculpture; in Italy it is relatively uncommon. It is quite possible that there is a connection between the visions of the great Spanish mystics, St. Teresa of Avila, for instance, and the stressing of this subject in sculpture. So strict was the spiritual background for the religious art of that country

Fig. 6.   THE MISSION IN 1865

that exact instructions were given for the execution of works. The iconography was prescribed in detail; the Crucified had to be nailed to the cross with four rather than three nails and with the feet crossed. He was to be presented before death, with the head turned to the right side, the eyes were to be open and the face filled with strong emotion. Montañés carried out these instructions and in spite of painting streams of blood and the real drapery on the loins, he created a classically perfect and beautiful body.

Similarly, Montañés' *Inmaculadas* are more quiet, more in keeping with the serenity of the classical Greek than with the extravagances of Juni and Hernández. His follower, Alonso Cano, produced what may be the prototypes of many Mexican *Inmaculadas*. Curiously, the even more reserved Sorrowful Mother type created by Becerra and made popular by Mora (1642-1724), with its restrained humility and resignation, never was very popular in Mexican sculpture. The type is Italian rather than Spanish in feeling.

Cedar, lime, and the hard wood known as *alerce* were frequently employed for sculpture, though preference was given to the Sorian pine. The coloring was sometimes laid on canvas with which the figure was covered, and the effects and gradations of tints were as carefully applied as in paintings. Real draperies were generally used for single figures, especially those of the Madonna. In these cases only the heads and the extremities were finished, the rest of the statue being left a mere mannequin or block of wood. More frequently, the cloth of the drapery was dipped in a solution of gesso, or plaster, then molded into shape around the figure. Upon drying, the garment hardened, and since the wood sculpture itself was completely covered with a layer of gesso, the parts became virtually indistinguishable. The proper colors were subsequently applied.

In Mexico, the sculpture of this later period received specialized treatment. The saints were invariably carved by special figure sculptors. The carving was, in many cases, covered by a thin layer of fine gold leaf applied over gesso, and then burnished. The faces and hands received a treatment known as *encarnación,* either shiny or dull. A process known as *estofado* was used on clothing: a stenciling device that colored in the pattern and left the remainder gold. Quite frequently, real eyelashes were used on glass eyes, and often, real teeth.[7]

By the middle of the seventeenth century, the art of painting flourished in Mexico. The schools benefited from the prosperity of the colony; the churches were filled with pictures of all sizes. The pictorial ideals in Mexico remained the same as those of the mother country, for new artists kept arriving from the Old World, and continued to

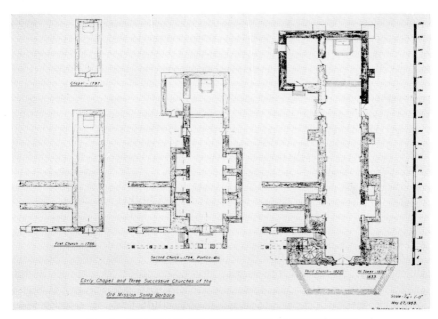

Fig. 7.   DIAGRAM OF SUCCESSIVE MISSION SITES
(by Thaddeus Kreye, O.F.M.)

mould style and taste in the New. Portraits and religious pictures were the principal subjects for the painters. Up to the end of the century the styles were essentially classical in spirit, whether Flemish, Italian, or Spanish in manner. The Baroque painting of the later period in Mexico began with the introduction of the style, especially of Ribalta, Herrera, Zurbarán, and Ribera—a vigorous art of strong light and dark patterns and rather restricted or limited color schemes, contrasting markedly with the more brilliant color schemes of the Italian schools. However, the lack of bright color was incompatible with the Mexican spirit and the low-keyed paintings gave way to those of brighter hue. The result was a combination of strong light and dark modeling with the softer, more luminous color of the earlier style.

It is an unexplainable and curious fact that the intense religiosity of El Greco had little or no influence on either Spanish or Mexican religious painting. Assuredly his work was replete with the very mysticism so characteristic of the Spanish religious; unquestionably this absence of influence may be attributed to the lack of the realistic and attainable sentiment that seemed to be demanded by even the members of the religious orders.

Much more influential was Herrera, whose rather matter-of-fact "visions" and other religious paintings were easily understood. The same was true of Zurbarán, whose deeper and more subtle emotion was coupled with a strong feeling for structure in his figures, as well as with incisive lighting. Naturalism and "tenebroso" (an indefinite cloudy shading) were the two principal characteristics that influenced much of Mexican painting, and more frequently, were directly copied. Velázquez was rarely copied, possibly because he had painted so few religious works. Ribera, however, appealed largely because in the case of his scenes of martyrdom, the factual and the attention to realistic detail were more in keeping with the generally narrative tendencies of liturgical art.

Murillo without question was the greatest popular painter of religious subject matter in Spain, especially of the various representations of the *Inmaculada*. He was the great narrative painter of Spanish art. His mature works were all imbued with a charm and grace and tenuous beauty that appealed to the sentimental. A great many Mexican paintings are copies, or rather adaptations, of Murillo's style. None, however, attained that peculiar individuality of his. Toward the end of the seventeenth century the work of Valdés Leal, who somewhat imitated Murillo but who nevertheless produced works of considerable power and wealth of color, became very popular in Mexico.

Still another fairly strong influence was that of Rubens, whose work first appeared in Mexico in the form of engravings and copies. Much of the subsequent work in Mexico reveals a great variety of the foregoing influences and is for the most part quite uneven in value. Finally, by the end of the century, a small group of artists in Mexico developed still another style characterized by gracefulness. Figures were more lyrical; landscapes had a bluish tinge or a golden one—a quality rather ethereal and very typically and purely Mexican in style.

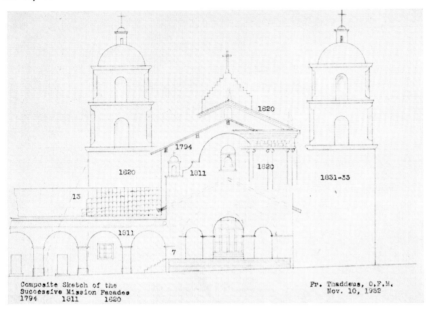

Fig. 8. COMPOSITE SKETCH OF THE MISSION FACADES
(by Thaddeus Kreye, O.F.M.)

The sculpture of this later Baroque period was similarly varied; most single religious sculptures had robes of brocade on gold grounds, with delicate flesh tints for the face and hands.

The true European Baroque architecture gave way to the sometimes rather fantastic Churrigueresque style, in which movement, rhythm, and fantasy of expression dominated. In Mexico it became "a religious art in its anxiety to make the house of God not only as splendid as possible but also a celestial vision." Serra built churches of this type, though on a simpler scale, in the remote Sierra Gorda region. One finds in a limited sense an imitation of these fabulous exteriors and interiors in several of the California Missions. The theatrical draperies, curtains, and arches that in the Santa Barbara and several other missions are now painted devices, existed as stone carvings in many Mexican Baroque churches, both inside and outside the buildings.

During the eighteenth century the production of paintings in Mexico was enormous, for the demand was great. Studios consequently turned out hundreds of canvases, most of which lacked character. The great influence of the early period was above all Murillo, but neither his realism nor the spiritual quality of his work was taken over. Rather, it was the conventions of coloring and of form. Three or four tints were repeated monotonously; faces were invariably rose, drapery was blue or red, backgrounds grey or ochre. By the end of the century hundreds of copies, monotonously even in quality and almost totally lacking in artistic merit, of virtually every engraving that arrived in Mexico, were made in identical pictures.

Mexico City, when Alexander von Humboldt reached it in March, 1803, was already an old city and a remarkable one, with many fine establishments devoted to science and the fine arts:

> . . . a fine arts academy . . . owing its existence to the liberality of private citizens and the protection of Minister Galves . . . and a collection of plaster casts finer than anything of the kind in Germany. . . . In this academy instruction was free, and were found studying and competing all, Indian and white, whom talent and opportunity favored, for art is nature, and makes the whole world kin, knowing no aristocracy but that of genius. The excellent instruction supplied by this school has already great influence on the architectural taste of the nation. . . .[8]

This Academia de las Nobles Artes (the San Carlos Academy) had been founded in 1781-1783 as a school of engraving, and three years later it was enlarged to include instruction in the other arts. From the time of its founding the Spanish King Carlos III gave the academy strong support; the best teachers and models were sent over from Spain; the casts mentioned by Humboldt were a personal gift sent over in 1791.

It must have been rather a remarkable experience for the early British and American travelers to California to enter into one of the adobe and stone churches during the years from 1795 to 1840. In what were tiny settlements in an oasis of farming surrounded by virgin country, the mission churches afforded the only link with an old European culture. Sculpture and paintings that were logical to the neo-classic and baroque of Europe must have looked rather illogical in the necessarily simple, and at times rather crude, adobe churches of California.

Nowhere else in America can one find collections of works that had in essence not only a decorative but a social value and importance. The famous world traveler, Jean François Gilaup de La Pérouse, visited the Mission San Carlos (Carmel) in 1786, when the church still had a straw roof, and wrote of the decorations:

> . . . The parish church is very clean, although covered with thatch; it is dedicated to Charles and ornamented with rather good paintings, copied from originals in Italy. One sees there a picture of hell, in which the painter seems to have borrowed a bit from the imagination of Callot; but as it is absolutely necessary to impress vividly the senses of the new converts, I am persuaded that such a representation was never more useful in any country, and that it would be impossible for the Protestant religion, which proscribes images, and almost all the other ceremonies of our Church, to make any progress among those people. I have my doubts that the picture of Paradise, which is placed opposite the picture of Hell, produces on them as good an effect; the state of quietism which it represents, and that sweet satisfaction of the elect who surround the throne of the Supreme Being, are ideas too sublime for rude, coarse men, but it was necessary to place rewards by the side of the punishments, and it was a strict duty not to permit any change in the kind of joys which the Catholic religion promises.[9]

La Pérouse's observations regarding the actual function of the paintings in the Church were nothing new, for the Church had used art as a means of social control for centuries. It helped considerably for the illiterate of the early Middle Ages to see pictured for him the good life and the glorious rewards, as well as the probable punishments of an unrepentant, wicked life. That these pictures and sculptures were to a certain extent the expressions of the artists goes without saying, yet it was all directed, prescribed, and supported by the Church. It had nothing to do with the superstition which the Church had always fought; it had a very great deal to do with contemplation. Just how the primitive Indians first reacted to the paintings can well be imagined. For them, pictorial expression had been rather limited to symbolic and semi-abstract pictographs in an extremely limited range of colors, without much regard for story or subject matter and with only the rudiments of what is called "pictorial composition." Examples of this type of expression can be found in some caves of the California Coast Ranges.

Father Zephyrin Engelhardt, writing of the founding of Mission San Gabriel on September 9, 1771, tells how Fathers Somera and Cambon

> . . . suddenly found themselves surrounded by a numerous band of armed savages. Fearing an attack, and not knowing what else to do, one of the friars unfurled a banner, which on one side showed the

picture of Our Lady of Sorrows, and held it up to the gaze of the howling Indians. No sooner had the gentiles set their eyes on the image of the Blessed Virgin than they threw down their bows and arrows. . . . The Indians from all the neighboring rancherias . . . gazed in wonder and delight at the holy Virgin.[10]   (See Figures 2 and 3.)

There was absolutely no basis for comparison as far as the Indians were concerned. Hence, the early fathers were confronted with a very serious problem, that of idolatry. At first, beyond the Crucifix and the altar cards, there were probably very few paintings or statues—perhaps a few banners and small sculptures. But as the Indians came to understand something of the nature of the faith, the traditional embellishments of the churches, at first but rude chapels, increased. The following quotation from the journal of Duhaut-Cilly, the French navigator who visited Santa Barbara in March, 1827, is a case in point:

Fig. 9.   DOORWAY TO THE TOWER

In art it [the stone fountain in front of the Mission building] is
imperfect, but still it caused so much the more surprise the less we
expected to find in this land so distant from the comforts of Europe,
an ornament or species of luxury which among ourselves is reserved only
for the places of the most wealthy.[11]

That the painting collections were impressive to the traveler is
borne out in the brief mention made by J. M. Letts in his journal,
California Illustrated. He visited Santa Barbara in December of 1850,
and among other things, wrote:

It is a small town, hardly deserving the name, and has acquired its name
and importance from its mission, the mission house being a building
of great capacity, containing a collection of valuable paintings. The front
makes some pretentions to architectural beauty, with two towers, each
containing two bells; between the towers is a representation of the sun,
the disc being the dial of a clock.[12] (Figure 4.)

In Santa Barbara, as early as 1797, the Fourteen Stations of the
Cross were brought from Mexico to the Mission. These particular
works, as is the case in the majority of other paintings, may be
originals, adaptations, or copies of masters; with few exceptions their
like can be seen only in the California missions. Unfortunately a
very considerable number of the paintings are in very poor condition.
The larger pieces had been removed from their stretchers and folded
several times to facilitate transportation, probably in chests for ship
or donkey freight. Along the fold lines the paint has cracked badly.
Others have been buffeted about and are bruised, torn, dented. The
majority have years of accumulated grime that has dulled some colors
almost beyond recognition. Still further damage to the paintings
has resulted from rigorous washing. Funds should be made available
for the careful cleaning and restoration of these historically important
pieces. But through this grime and yellowing, through the abrasions,
cracks and other damage, the paintings speak out from the cool walls
of the mission churches for the greater glory of God.

The paintings and sculpture in the Santa Barbara Mission have
been acquired at irregular intervals over a period of years from 1797
to the present. Some were "commissioned" through San Fernando
Convent in Mexico, headquarters for the Spanish missionary padres,
or from the convent of Zacatecas, with direct specifications as to
subject matter and destination;[13] others have been the gifts of parish-
ioners; still others have come from other missions or institutions.
Unfortunately for posterity, the Franciscan missionaries in California
kept no truly accurate records of their possessions, save in the case
of the souls entrusted to their care. Hence, the origin or acquisition

of paintings, sculpture, and vestments, and in many cases even data concerning buildings that were constructed is difficult to determine. Frequently only casual or brief mention of a work was entered in the records or inventories, and this lack makes the task of chronology and exact identification an extremely difficult one, with the result that conclusions arrived at with all due care might in many cases be open to question. Until such time in the future when, it is hoped, more specific records and inventories may be brought to light, the interpretation and classification of the works is at best a rather arbitrary one. Furthermore, the practice of lending or giving of pictures and other objects to missions in need of them, for one or another reason (and frequently without mention in the records), was very common and in fact exists at the present time. Finally, much material in the missions has disappeared during the last century.

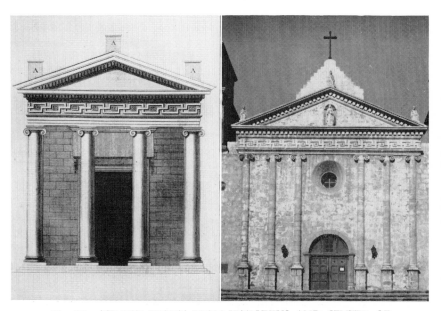

Fig. 10.   TEMPLE FRONT FROM VITRUVIUS AND CENTER OF
FACADE OF THE MISSION

Much of the loss and the eventual dismemberment of the missions began as early as 1810 with the Hidalgo revolt in Mexico. In 1813 the Spanish government passed a "secularization act" which, however, was not enforced. This act would have put the entire system of missions under the jurisdiction of the Mexican bishop. With the cutting off of the Pious Fund,[14] the Franciscan college in that country became unable to provide the annual stipends for the padres. The funds accumulated were confiscated by the government and used for other purposes. In addition, the missions were called upon to support territorial soldiers and guards; virtually all the food and most of the equipment had to be provided.

In 1821 Mexico proclaimed its independence from the mother country. The machinations of the Spanish Cortes against the religious orders had at last effectually estranged the American colonies from Spain. During the ensuing quarrel over Mexican independence, the missions at first steadfastly maintained their loyalty to Spain, and many padres left the country rather than to take the oath of allegiance to the new Mexican government. Subsequently, in 1827, all native Spaniards were banished. At first an empire was set up, then a republic, and the political and economic unrest in Mexico severely affected the welfare of all the missions. California became a dependency of Mexico, no longer subject to Spain, and the elements of disorder and irreligion soon came to the fore. Real "freedom" was not established. Indian revolts, conflicts between the soldiers and natives, and financial problems plagued the missions constantly in spite of their wealth. From the time of the Mexican independence, the welfare of the missions declined.

In January of 1831 an illegal and revolutionary proclamation by the wily Mexican governor of California, Echeandía "freed" all

Fig. 11.   ENTRANCE TO THE MONASTERY, 1882

the Indians in the Monterey, San Diego, and Santa Barbara presidial districts, that is, all those who were qualified to become Mexican citizens. The properties of the missions were to be confiscated. There followed several years of political chicanery and intrigue; attempts to ameliorate the deplorable situation among the Indians and the missions in order to counteract the greed of the "revolutionary" government were desultory. This disastrous secularization law which gave to the Indians their complete freedom, and which took over their properties as well as those of the missions, was subsequently passed by the Mexican Congress in August of 1833.[15] Mexico was in a constant state of turmoil or revolution; governor after governor came to California. From 1836 to 1842, under Alvarado, there was only plunder and ruin. From that time on the missions were objects of legalized pillage; everything of value was removed. The buildings were allowed to fall into ruin; under Pico they were rented or sold. The padres remained in a few churches. In others they were replaced by secular priests who were but meagerly paid. In the mad scramble before the American occupation everything was sold for what it would bring. Records were destroyed; church goods, including books, paintings, sculpture, vestments, and altar accessories were bought, stolen, and scattered. Some found their ways into private homes; some disappeared altogether.

Fortunately Santa Barbara escaped the total, or near total, destruction that was the fate of several of the missions, and it became the depository for many records and books. At the time of the secularization in 1834 the church was valued at $16,000.00, the sacristy at $1,500.00, the "ornaments" and library together at $4,728.00. Although very nearly all of its secular possessions were lost, it remained in the control of the Franciscans. It was never so completely abandoned or misused as were the other missions. It was during this period of decline that Bishop García Diego lived at the Mission. He retained the principal building for himself and for the padres. Some attempts were made in 1843 to restore the mission system, but the conditions set forth were untenable. In 1845 all the buildings except the church and the monastery were leased for the sum of $1,200.00 a year, from which income the bishop, the padres, and the surviving Indians were supported. In 1846 Pico sold the Mission for $7,500.00; later litigation annulled the sale.

Also in 1846, Santa Barbara came under the jurisdiction of the United States. Since that time there have been no annoyances such as existed under Mexican rule. Eventually a considerable portion of the properties: the churches, monasteries, gardens, cemeteries, and the like were returned to the Catholic Church. The beginning of an apostolic college at Santa Barbara was made in 1853 for the training of Franciscans. In 1865 the Mission received a patent from Abraham Lincoln, and some three hundred acres were restored. The old Mission was for years the mother house of the Franciscan Province at St. Barbara on the Pacific coast; it is now a parish church and a theological seminary, as well as the archive center for historical studies of the Order. Early in the twentieth century public interest in the missions as historical landmarks was aroused, and considerable progress has been made toward the restoration of many of the missions in the state.

The Old Mission
at
Santa Barbara

The Old Mission at Santa Barbara

Santa Barbara, the town and the Mission, as well as the entire area of the Channel Islands, was given its name by three Carmelite friars [1] who accompanied the Spanish explorer Sebastián Vizcaíno in 1602 on his exploratory voyage up the coast of California. As was the custom at that time, any discovery of a land, bay, or the founding of a township, fort, or mission, was made in the name of the Spanish king. A place name was immediately assigned. Frequently the name of a saint on whose anniversary or feast day the discovery was made, or in whose honor an expedition was undertaken, was given to the place. Actually, the name Santa Barbara was given to the Channel and to one of the islands because the first passage was made on December 3, 1602, the eve of the feast of St. Barbara. A favorable wind had come up after seven months of storms and adverse winds, the first since leaving Acapulco. In thanksgiving they christened it El Canal de Santa Barbara. First mention of the name in the history of the coast was entered in the account of that passage by the Franciscan historian, Father Juan de Torquemada in his *Monarchia Indiana*. The name Canal de St. Barbara [*sic*] is shown on a Briggs type map of 1625. Of the site of Santa Barbara Vizcaíno noted: "It is fertile, for it has pine groves and oaks, and a fine climate, for though it gets cold, it is not so cold as to cause discomfort."

Not until 1768 was the occupation and preparation for the colonizing of Alta California ordered by the Spanish crown, and the following year the expedition under Gaspar de Portolá and Father Junípero Serra set out from Mexico. That same year, on July 16, 1769, San Diego Mission was founded, the first of the twenty-one missions in Alta California.

Seventeen years later, on December 4, 1786, on the Feast of St. Barbara, the Mission at Santa Barbara was founded. The Presidio and community had been established in April, 1782, and Father Serra erected there a chapel, blessed and dedicated "the land to God our Lord." Because of the friction between Serra and the Governor of California, Felipe de Neve, the actual founding of the Mission proper did not take place until after Father Serra's death. In 1785, when Father Fermín Lasuén became Father Presidente, preparations finally got under way. The formal dedication of the first mission chapel, some distance north of the Presidio took place on December 16, 1786, in the name of the Catholic King of Spain, Don Carlos III, in the

27

presence of the new Governor, Pedro Fages, and Father Lasuén. The formal founding of the Mission and the erection of some sort of habitation was forbidden by the Governor until he himself would be present. The name for the new mission had been selected by Viceroy Martín de Mayorga on December 7, 1780, along with Purísima Concepción and San Buenaventura.[2] However, December 4, the day on which the Cross was raised on the site of the future mission, was always regarded as the day of the founding. Father Lasuén closed the first part of the title page of the baptismal register with: "May it be for the greater honor and glory of God, the exaltation of His most holy name, and the welfare of souls."[3]

Fig. 12.   THE MISSION IN 1883 (from an etching by H. C. Ford)

Like all first structures in California, this chapel was merely a crude hut, a palisade-walled enclosure, the interstices of the wooden stakes being plastered with clayey mud. The roof was flat and made of branches with a thatch of grass and tules. There was neither time nor material nor sufficient labor to erect a more permanent building. None of the missions built before 1790 were of good construction; the buildings were none other than extremely primitive affairs. There were no bell towers, no stone or tile work, and no arches.

Early in 1787 construction of the semi-permanent mission buildings was begun, with Fathers Antonio Paterna and Cristóbal Oramas

Fig. 13.   THE HIGH ALTAR, ABOUT 1874

as the priests in charge. In addition to living quarters, kitchens, store-rooms, dormitories, and the like, the first chapel, thirty-nine feet long and fourteen feet wide, was built. Except for one later building constructed of adobe, the others, including the chapel, were built of poles (timbers) and interwoven brush, faced with clay, and with thatched roofs, similar to the huts of the Indians. By the end of the following year (1788) an addition built of adobe, possibly the sanctuary, was made to the chapel, and tile was first made by the Indians for the roofing to replace the inflammable thatched roofs. The Mission compound was beginning to take the form of a quadrangle.

The next year (1789) a new church seventeen feet wide and one hundred and eight feet long was constructed of adobe and roofed with tiles. The interior was embellished with a new table for the altar, a new tabernacle, and a fresh set of altar cards. The first true mission altar and tabernacle were made of wood, the work of the Indians. It is now in one of the museum rooms and is fully described in the catalogue. This new church was not, as is generally supposed, an enlargement of the first, but was a new structure save possibly for the earlier well-constructed adobe sanctuary.

Several other buildings of considerable size, all of adobe with tile roofs, were constructed—apartments, two or more storerooms, and so on, so necessary for the mission community. In that year, 1789, a statue of St. Anthony of Padua was acquired. It is possible that this work, which Father Engelhardt mentions as being about three feet in height, is the one now in the museum. If this be so, it is the oldest extant work in the Mission. The records give its acquisition as April 1, 1790.

Because of the lack of skilled workmen in the province, Governor Fages in the fall of 1790 requested of the officials in Mexico a considerable number of artisans and teachers, as well as a surveyor. Expert masons were needed for the stone churches to be built at Santa Barbara and at Carmel, San Gabriel, San Buenaventura, and San Juan Capistrano.

In 1793 the third church since the founding of the Mission was begun. The old one proved too small for the ever growing congregation of neophytes. This time it was a considerably larger one, the dimensions being twenty-five by one hundred and twenty-four feet, with an adjoining sacristy fourteen by twenty-six, in all probability to the west of the sanctuary. Unlike the earlier structures, this was better finished, being plastered inside and out with mortar and roofed with tiles. Father Antonio Paterna, the builder of the Mission, died on the thirteenth of February of that year, not living to see the completion of his dream. The new church was dedicated on March 19, 1794, on the Feast of St. Joseph and endured until the disastrous earthquake of December, 1812. This third church was considerably more splendid than the others had been; there were six side chapels, or oratories, three on each side. These were probably similar to the present Chapels of St. Francis and St. Anthony.

Recent demolition and excavation work has produced conclusive evidence that the church of 1793-1794 was standing on the site of its successor. The south wall of the 1789 church coincided with that of the two later ones, and the original west or end wall was in line with the steps of the present sanctuary. At that time the north (opposite) wall was some seventeen feet out, making a church seventeen feet wide and one hundred and seven feet long. In 1794 that width was extended to twenty-five feet, and the side chapels added. The roof of this church was about eight feet higher than the first one.

Fig. 14. THE MISSION CHURCH INTERIOR, 1880

Parts of the original (1793) façade and arcade, buttress, and entrance platform have recently been discovered.

The façade of this church was located on a line with the front of the "padres' building" with the arcade or corridor extending forward from it. The façade was some twelve feet back of the present (1820) and much more elaborate front. The entrance vestibule or portico was added to the front in 1811. It was made of brick and also roofed with tiles.

In 1795 two statues, one of the Immaculate Conception and the other of St. Joseph, were acquired by Fathers Tapis and Miguel for the interior.[4]

In 1796 the front corridor facing the Presidio was built, measuring nine feet wide and some one hundred and twenty-four feet long. The pillars were of brick and mortar and the roof of tiles; this corridor served to protect the adobe wall of the mission structure from the rains, which, when they came, were generally from the southeast. This arcade extended to the very edge of the 1820 church; parts of arches and pillars as well as other evidence was uncovered during the present work. The last three arches were subsquently imbedded in the west tower and the adjoining buttress. The appearance of the mission church at that time was perhaps similar to that of the present look of St. Francis Solano (Sonoma Mission), excepting that the position of the church is at the opposite end of the corridor. (The Sonoma Mission is fairly well preserved but is now a heterogeneous museum).

In 1797 the Mission acquired the Fourteen Stations of the Cross, all of which can be seen on the walls of the nave at the present time. Six large oil paintings were acquired in 1798.[5] Besides these, two Crucifixes were added, each about twenty-five inches tall, and a bell weighing 375 pounds was secured. This year also, great progress was made with many new buildings: granaries, shops, and dormitories, as well as an Indian village of nineteen adobe houses built outside of the new well-established square of the Mission compound proper.

On December 31, 1801, three statues, one of Our Lady of Sorrows, one of St. Michael, and one of St. Francis, each about three feet high, were acquired. The St. Michael is the seventeenth-century piece of polychromed wood now in the private upstairs chapel. A similar but larger work of St. Michael is in the museum, though in the invoice of 1858 it is listed as "a holy guardian angel."[6] It is about forty-two inches high. The Our Lady of Sorrows is now on a small altar at the east end of the upstairs gallery in the living quarters of the padres.

Fig. 15. THE MISSION CHURCH INTERIOR, 1890

The next year "a silver crown, gold plated" was obtained for the statue of the Immaculate Conception, also a silver halo for the statue of St. Joseph, and finally, a small silver crown for the statue of the Infant Jesus.[7] This is the Infant being held by St. Joseph.

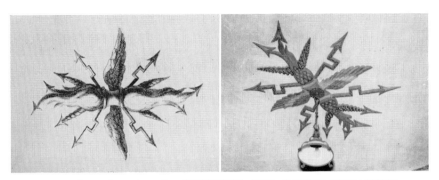

Fig. 16. DETAILS FROM VITRUVIUS AND CEILING ORNAMENT

No mention has been made of the windows or other openings in the church, but in 1808 glass was provided for the fenestration of both the Sacristy and the church. In that year, for the first time, a building was erected for the manufacture of pottery. A new masonry front for the Mission building, consisting of another row of larger rooms all along the corridor facing the Presidio, and with a flat roof of "polished concrete," was begun during 1808 and finished in 1811. When this row of rooms (the apartments for the fathers and guests) was completed, the corridor with its massive pillars of brick, stone arches, and a floor of tiles was built. The roof of the corridor served as an open porch. The façade (portico) of the church itself was finished, but there is no record of any description of its appearance. The ornate Moorish style fountain in front of the Mission was also built in 1808.

The terrible earthquake of December 21 [1812] and the days that followed have damaged the Mission to such an extent that all the buildings will have to be closely examined and more or less repaired, especially the church edifice, in place of which, after permission is obtained from the Government, a new building will certainly have to be erected; because comparing the labor necessary to repair it with the work of the new edifice, the difference will be small; and comparing the little satisfaction which repaired walls would give us with the security which new and strong walls on a solid foundation would provide, the reasons for the latter will outweigh the former. This plan is accordingly decided upon.[8]

Permission to build the new church was finally received in 1815. The fathers were not entirely free to follow their taste and ambition in the erection of church buildings, for royal decrees placed certain restrictions on them. In the meantime, some repairs had been made to the damaged church so that services could be continued. The new church was erected under the supervision of Father Antonio Ripoll, and possibly with the assistance of one Señor Rocha, who had just finished his labors at the San Luis Rey church, and of the master mason, Martínez. The new building was erected partially on the site of the old one, for there is no evidence that a change was made anywhere. The three permanent churches of the Mission occupied the same spot: the northeast corner of the Mission quadrangle.[9]

Building over and around a "ruined" building (in this instance amounting also to enlarging and repairing) is sometimes still practiced, and it is possible that this was done in the case of Santa Barbara Mission. In 1817 the front half of the wing facing the Presidio, and which had had a flat roof, was remodeled with a new gable roof covered with tiles and enlarged to extend over both halves and the arches. Further extension of the old length of the church occurred in that the Reredos of the sanctuary was placed some thirteen feet back. This brought the total length of the church to its present 162½ feet. Fathers Francisco Suñer and Antonio Ripoll were justly proud of the splendid church they had built. It was dedicated on September 10, 1820:

> It is of dressed stone and mortar. The walls of solid sandstone of two varas, or nearly six feet thick, are strengthened by stone buttresses. The massive tower of the same material has two stories and holds six bells.[10]

Fig. 17.   CEILING ROSETTE AND STAR OF POLYCHROMED WOOD

It is clear that at the dedication only one of the towers was finished. The French traveler Duhaut-Cilly, when he visited Santa Barbara in 1827, wrote:

> As we proceeded, the Mission buildings looked more beautiful. . . . From the bay you might have mistaken it for a mediaeval castle with its high windows, its tower and its watch-tower; but on approaching it . . . it takes on little by little a religious appearance. The turret becomes a belfry; . . . the castle is a convent . . . one is astonished at the boldness of the design and the firmness of its execution; nothing but a boundless zeal for the spread of religion has enabled Padre Ripoll to be victorious over so many obstacles.[11]

Recent [12] discoveries of papers and other evidence have clarified the "mystery" of the date of the two towers. The oldest is the south tower, nearest the monastery. Conclusive evidence points to the fact that this tower and the imposing façade were constructed in one operation. Hence the outer wall of the tower and the front of the church were continuous. The winding stairs within the tower were built as the tower went up, and all empty space was filled with rubble. The heavy buttress to the south of the tower was put up at a much later time, probably in 1857 after the earthquake of that year. The second, or northern, tower was erected in 1831, but because of faulty construction it collapsed shortly thereafter. Finally, in 1832 the fallen one was rebuilt, more solidly than at first and blessed (probably) on January 15, 1833. Alfred Robinson, describing his visit early in the 1840's mentions: "The floor of colored cement . . . the walls painted and hung round with pictures of saints . . . a door led into the church, where we behold a gorgeous display of banners, paintings, images, and crucifixes of gold and silver."[13] As to the exterior: "The stone church, with its two towers and extensive wing, its artificial clock, tiled roofs, arched corridors, and majestic fountain was before us."[14] Yet in 1903 in a pamphlet about the Mission, John Bodkin mentions only one tower: "The bell tower contains two old bells properly inscribed. . . ."[15]

The towers of nearly all the missions differ from their Mexican and Spanish prototypes in their great massiveness, the simplicity of detail, and the almost universal use of the dome on top. There seems to be no explanation for the use of the dome in preference to the steeple or pyramidal roof excepting tradition: the Moorish influence and the use of that "half-orange" shape since the tenth century on the Spanish peninsula.

All the early sketches show the twin towers complete, and du Mofras and other early writers also mention them. The bells generally

Fig. 18.   PAINTED DOOR FRAME
DECORATIONS

Fig. 19.   PAINTED WINDOW
DECORATIONS

came from Lima, Peru, and from Mexico. Because of the architectural
distinction of the two towers, Santa Barbara is generally considered the
finest and most graceful of the missions. The façade, flanked by the
square towers of three tiers, is ornamented by six slender engaged
columns derived from the Greek Ionic order. In the center niche
(typanum) of the triangular pediment surmounting the columns was
a statue of St. Barbara, carved from native stone, and colored. The
apex and the angles of the pediment were also adorned with statues
representing Faith, Hope, and Charity. These three were damaged
beyond repair when they toppled from the pediment during the
earthquake of June 29, 1925. The fragments are now in the museum.
Above the pediment is a stepped gable supporting the Cross.

The design of the entire façade was based on details of the
classic Ionic order as illustrated in the Spanish translation of Vitruvius'
book on architecture, which is still in the Mission library. Father
Ripoll had necessarily modified the Ionic details with a blend of both
Spanish and so-called Moorish architectural features. The translation
by Father O'Keefe of the Padre's account best describes the interior
as it was around 1820:

> The interior is neatly finished: the walls are plastered; the columns and
> the cornices are frescoed; the ceiling is lathed, hard finished, ornamented
> with designs from Vitruvius, cut from cedar and painted. The floor of
> red cement, made from oil and lime, is hard and finely polished. The altars
> are neatly ornamented with crucifixes and statues in wood. Over the
> high altar, on a bracket in the wall, stands a statue of Santa Barbara. On
> each side of Santa Barbara is a painting on the canvas wall piece of
> St. Joachim and of St. Anne. Directly under these on brackets are the

statues in wood of the Blessed Virgin and of St. Joseph. Small wooden
statues of St. Dominic and of St. Francis may be seen on each side of
the High Altar, on pillars.[16]

There were no seats, or pews, in the early California churches.
People brought mats, small rugs, or even stools. For a description
of the Mission, Duhaut-Cilly's account, written on the occasion of
his visit in 1827, is of great interest, for in the intervening hundred
years to the time of the 1925 earthquake, few changes excepting
deterioration took place:

> . . . the long atrium or cloister [is] supported by fifteen square pillars
> which were formed into fourteen arches . . . these gave the Mission a
> noble appearance, which on our arrival surprised us. . . . The front of
> the church is ornamented with six half-columns that support a triangular
> façade furnished with a few statues of saints. The interior of the
> church consists only of a nave with a flat ceiling and with no side
> entrances. The form of the building would cause no special wonder if
> it had been constructed by the Europeans; but considering that it is the
> work of poor Indians under the direction of an ecclesiastic; that it is a
> building raised in a country which . . . offers materials only in the
> crude, natural state . . . surely then one admires very much the great
> patience of the religious, his ability, and the care he exercises in conducting
> the work . . . the boldness of the conception and the constancy in its
> execution are striking. No motive, except his unbounded zeal for the
> spread of Religion, could have sustained Padre Ripoll . . . the nave,
> the altar, and the sacristy are hung with paintings, the best of which
> come from Mexico, the rest of them are the work of Indian hands. The
> pillars, the trimmings, the cornice work, and the plinths have a rather
> tasteful marble finish, and are decorated with arabesques by hands not
> altogether unskilled.[17]

Further reconstruction and enlargement of the padres' building
took place in 1850. An additional series of rooms was built over
the front corridor, extending about half the length of the building.
The remaining half of the "front" rooms, extending to the end of
the convento building, were added in 1860. Because of the "concrete"
floor of the corridor roof over which these rooms were placed, a
wooden floor was laid the entire length of the second floor, resulting
in a considerable difference in levels between the rooms facing on the
inner quadrangle, the central hall, and the new rooms. The construction of these front rooms was much lighter and less sturdy than that
of the ground floor, and the entire upper story suffered severe damage
in the 1925 earthquake.

In some photographs dating from about 1882 (see Figure 11),
there is a very interesting pattern visible near the base of this upper
story. At the height where the original balustrade of the balcony

must have been is a repetition of two closed arches, and one triangular form, contiguous to each other. Above this border or balustrade, and in between the arches and triangles, the bricks of the wall can clearly be seen where the plaster had fallen away. There is considerable difference between the quality of the plaster on the "balustrade" and that which covered the bricks, the latter appearing much smoother. Two explanations may be suggested for the pattern. When, in 1850, the rooms were added, the new walls were merely built on top of the thick balustrade, with spaces left for window openings. This could have been done, although the construction was certainly not very sound. Another explanation for the design running along the wall is that it was intended to be just that: an ornamental device, probably in low relief and of stucco or plaster, to relieve the monotony of the building front.[18]

Fig. 20.   PILASTER-BASE DESIGNS

In March, 1861, William H. Brewer of the Whitney Geological Survey visited the Mission during his exploration of the state of California. His account of the appearance of the Mission is illuminating:

. . . A wealthy Mission formerly existed here, but like all the rest, is now poor after the robbery by the Mexican Government. I have not seen before in America, except at Panama, such extensive ruins. . . . We went into the church—a fine old building, about 150 feet long (inside), 30 wide, and 40 high, with two towers, and a monastery, sacristy, etc., 250 feet long at one side, with long corridors and stone pillars and small windows and tile roof. The interior of the church was striking and picturesque. Its walls were painted by the Indians who built it. The cornice and ornaments on the ceiling were picturesque indeed—the colors bright and the design a sort of cross between arabesques, Greek cornice, and Indian designs, yet the effect was pretty. The light streamed in through the small windows in the thick walls, lighting up the room. The floor was of cement. The sides and ceilings were plastered with the usual accompaniment of old pictures, shrines, images, altar, etc. The pictures were dingy with age, the tinsel and gilt of the images dull and tarnished by time and neglect. Some of the pictures were of considerable merit; such were two, one of the Crucifixion and another of the Conception.

On either side of the door, beneath the choir, were two old Mexican paintings: one of the martyrs calm and resigned in fire; the other, the damned in hell. The latter showed a lurid furnace of fire, the victims, held by iron bars, tormented by devils of every kind. In front was the drunkard with empty glass in his hand, a devil with the head of a hog pouring liquid fire from a bottle. The gambler, ready to clutch the money and the cards, was held back by a demon no less ugly. An old bald-headed man stood with a fighting cock in his hand, but tormented now. A woman had a serpent twined about her and feeding upon her breast, another was stung by scorpions.

Although the picture attracted the attention and imagination it had none of the merits of Rubens' "Descent of the Damned"! The victims had not that expression of remorse and anguish which he could paint so well, nor the demons that fiendish diabolical expression he conceived and expressed.

The same was true of another picture of Judgment Day, the separation of the just from the unjust—an elaborate work of the imagination, but not good as a work of art. Much better was a picture of the Virgin with broken scales of justice in her hand, an angel on each side pointing and directing the penitents at her feet to her look and mercy.[19]

Father Joseph O'Keefe wrote a small handbook for the benefit of visitors in 1885, and the following excerpt indicates how frequently the paintings were moved about:

The interior is neatly finished, the walls are all plastered, the columns and cornice frescoed, the ceilings lathed, hard finished, and ornamented with designs from Vitruvius, cut from cedar and painted. The floor of red cement made from oil and lime, is hard and finely polished. The altars are neatly ornamented with fine crucifixes and statues in wood. Over the high altar on a bracket in the wall, stands a statue in wood of Santa Barbara: on each side . . . is a painting on the canvas wall piece of St. Joachim and St. Ann. Directly under these are the statues in wood of the Blessed Virgin and St. Joseph on brackets. Small wooden statues of St. Dominic and St. Francis may be seen, one on each side of the high altar on pillars. The Day of Judgment, a poor copy of Murillo in the "Escorial" in Spain . . . Facing this is a good painting of Our Lady of the Scapular. Outside the sanctuary, on the wall, hangs a large painting of the Assumption and Coronation of the Blessed Virgin, and facing it one of the same size of the Crucifixion. All the above works were brought from Mexico for this Mission in 1798, together with the fourteen stations which are hung along the walls at equal distances. During the last twenty years the Church has been adorned with several paintings. St. Francis Solano, called the Apostle of Peru, on a column; over a side altar hangs one of the Blessed Virgin of the Seven Dolors; below this is a good one of Our Lady of Guadalupe; in front of this is a St. Anthony of Padua and St. Catherine of Alexandria. Over the door of the Sacristy hangs a splendid copy of Rubens' Descent From the Cross. Inside the Sacristy, over the vestment drawers, can be seen a splendid painting, which represents, according to St. Anselm, the dress worn by Our Lord and Savior, as painted by St. Luke; another represents the baptism of Our Lord by St. John. The Ambulatory is hung with several old and very good paintings; on one canvas are seen the three Archangels, St. Michael, St. Gabriel, and St. Raphael, on another of the same size are St. Clare, St. Rose, and St. Agnes. Three represent respectively, St. Francis of Assisi, St. Bonaventure and St. Peter Nolascus, and one beautiful painting of Our Lady, under the appellation of Refuge of Sinners.[20]

In 1890, Mrs. Yda Addis Storke wrote her *Memorial and Biographical History* of Santa Barbara and Ventura Counties. Of the Mission she wrote:

Under its present aspect, [it] is still very picturesque, although at close range, something of its charm is lost through the results of "restoration," which has destroyed the creamy time-mellowed tints of the surfaces, and imparted a certain obtrusive and commonplace setness to its appearance. Nevertheless, in its architectural fitness, in its dimensions, and in its situation. . . . The Mission bears strong witness to the

Fig. 21. SIDE ALTAR DECORATIONS

Fig. 22. THE MISSION IN 1890

taste and judicial discrimination of the Padres. The building has a very oriental aspect, what with its long arcade and two twin towers. . . . At the left of the Church is a wing 130 feet long, with the pillars and arches of its corridor well preserved. . . . This probably went to decay less than any of the other missions, and it was, furthermore, put in repair for the celebration of the centennial of its founding. Masses and services are held regularly at the Mission, which is in charge of Rev. Joseph O'Keefe, who is accompanied by some three or four fathers and about a dozen lay brothers.[21]

John Bodkin described the Mission as it appeared in 1902-1903 as follows:

It has two chapels, besides four side altars . . .; on entering the front door, on the right side, is a chapel dedicated to Our Lady of Sorrows.[22] Over this chapel is a large and very old painting representing Hell. Immediately opposite, on the left hand, is a chapel dedicated to St. Francis. The large oil painting over this chapel, also from Indian times, represents Purgatory. The frescoing of this chapel remains as it was when the building was finished in 1820, as also the frescoing [?] of the ceiling of the church. The wood carvings on the ceiling of the church proper are also part of the original decorations. The floor is modern, having been put in by Father Romo, 1872-1884, over the original cement pavement . . .

On the right hand is an altar dedicated in honor of Our Lady of Guadalupe.[23] The oil painting above it is an exact copy of the original at Guadalupe. . . . Beyond, close to the Communion rail, is the little altar dedicated to the Sacred Heart of Jesus.

On the left hand side, opposite the altar of Guadalupe, is an altar dedicated in honor of St. Joseph. . . . Close to the railing, on the same side, is the little altar of the famous wonderworker, St. Anthony of Padua. . . .

The altar of Our Lady of Guadalupe contains authentic relics of the Boy Martyr, St. Adeodat, who died for the Faith in one of the first centuries after Christ. They were brought from Rome by Rt. Rev. Bishop Mora.

The first [large painting] on the right represents the Assumption of Our Lady; That on the opposite side pictures of the Crucifixion. The picture inside the Sanctuary rail, on the right represents Our Lady of the Scapular (Mt. Carmel), while that on the left shows The Last Judgment, a copy of the original in the Escurial [sic], in Spain.[24] On the right, or Epistle side of the Altar, is an oil painting representing The Descent From the Cross, while that on the left is a life size picture of Our Lord.[25]

Back and above the High Altar are old statues of the Blessed Virgin and St. Joseph, while over the Altar is a statue of St. Barbara. On pedestals on either side of the Altar are two statues, that of St. Francis on the left, and St. Dominic on the right. These statues are very old, the product of loving piety rather than of art.[26]

Fig. 23. THE MISSION CHURCH INTERIOR, ABOUT 1914

Perhaps the most spectacular part of any large Catholic church built in the Spanish tradition is the area immediately behind, above, or surrounding the high altar, if there be more than one in the nave. Whenever there is a screen, or as is the case in Santa Barbara and in the majority of California missions, a decorated wall behind the main or high altar, that decorated wall is known as a *reredos*. In some churches it rises directly in back of the altar, that is, the altar is built against the wall. In the Santa Barbara church there is a passageway behind the altar leading to the door opening into the sacristy. This Reredos reaches, as it frequently does elsewhere, to the ceiling of the church.

The Reredos in the Mission church of today is quite different in detail from that existing before 1925. It is not in any way, save in minor details, a restoration of the earlier one. From 1820 on, the entire wall (faced with wood that was covered with canvas painted to represent stone and marble) was divided into six areas surmounted by a painted (mural) frieze of heavy floral garlands held by two angels in the center and facing forward, two angels on each side facing forward and lifting up the garland, and, at the extreme right and left, by another pair of angels who are partly in profile. The Reredos proper was in two principal horizontal bands, the uppermost having the statue of St. Barbara in a center bracket with sculptural and architectural details enframing her. (Figures 14, 15 and 23.) On each side of her, also in niches with Roman (Vitruvian) details of both sculpture and architecture framing them, were the "lienzos," the painted canvas panels of St. Anne on the right and St. Joachim on the left. These were painted as realistically as possible to suggest sculpture in the round, much in the manner of stage settings. As a matter of fact, it is quite certain that the entire inspiration for the painting of architectural and sculptural details was derived from the previously mentioned Spanish translation of Vitruvius in the Mission library. At the time Vitruvius wrote his famous work in the first century B.C., that very type of wall painting and decoration was common practice in Rome and in the neighboring cities. Above and to the right and left of the two painted saints, and topping the pair of painted "marble pillars" which separated St. Barbara from them, were a pair of painted partially draped cupid-like figures; these were more characteristic of the Italian school of painting than of the Spanish. The painter of the architectural details and of these figures was much more skilled in technique than the executor of the heavy garland above it, or of the two saints.

Below St. Joachim and standing on a projecting bracket was the statute of the Blessed Virgin (*Purísima Concepción*). Framing her was a simple "marbleized" painted panel. Opposite her, below St. Anne, was the statue of St. Joseph with a similar background.

Fig. 24. THE MISSION CHURCH INTERIOR, 1920-1925

The border running along the top of the Reredos and extending along the walls of the church just below the ceiling was continuous. In general, the interior decoration of most of the mission churches, not only in California but in Arizona, New Mexico, and Texas, was very similar. The "murals," unless representing scenes or persons, were generally more geometric than realistic in style, and frequently (as at San Miguel and Santa Ines) assumes an all over wallpaper pattern. This geometric character of ornament was a Spanish inheritance from the Moors, who rarely used imitations of nature in their ornament. Floral patterns were used in profusion and with great ingenuity, but animals or man, never. The most common geometric design was that known as the "Franciscan border," or frieze. The same pattern is to be seen along the walls of the present church, but a new and more elaborate one now tops the rebuilt Reredos. In 1911 a new wooden ceiling with narrow boards running lengthwise was installed. At that time, the ceiling decorations were for some reason omitted, to be supplied at an unspecified later time.[27]

Between 1913 and 1925 an extremely elaborate altar in the Italianate style was in use. (Figure 23) At each end of the altar table were kneeling angels in white; there was an elaborately carved altar screen behind and above the tabernacle, which had a Gothic-like porch above it, and within which was the altar Crucifix. There were two niches, one on each side of the Crucifix, in which were set on the left the old statue of St. Francis and on the right, that of St. Dominic.

Hanging on the sanctuary wall and almost in the corner were two large lunette-shaped oil paintings, on the left that of the Last Judgment, and opposite, just over the tomb of Bishop Diego, the equally large painting of Our Lady of Mt. Carmel.[28] Farther down on the left wall, near the communion rail, hung the large oil painting of Christ. The communion rail, a simple wooden balustrade, was set back about two feet from the top of a flight of five steps that led up to the sanctuary from the main floor of the church. It terminated against a massive, rather elaborately carved wooden pedestal at each end. This was directly against the first supporting wall pier, or pillar, in the nave. Thus the actual sanctuary was not as deep as it is at the present time. On top of each of these pedestals was a statue. On the left was a version of St. Francis embracing the Crucified Christ, a realization sculpturally of one of Murillo's well-known paintings, The Vow of St. Francis; on the right was a statue of The Immaculate Heart of Mary.

The entire effect of the Reredos, and particularly since 1913 when the over-elaborate and quite incongruous altar was installed, was rather garish. Otherwise, it was fundamentally as it had been since its dedication in 1820. Such changes as the introduction of functional but extremely ugly lighting fixtures, and the changing of pictures and statuary throughout the nineteenth century to suit the changing tastes of the pastors, were, in the last analysis, minor ones. The photograph, Figure 23, was taken between 1913 and 1925.

There has been considerable argument and much literature concerning the "interior decoration" of the missions. That most of the padres knew little of drawing and perhaps less of color effects is true. They originated nothing new in the way of decoration, largely because of their limited skill and lack of knowledge of the arts. Quite possibly their memories of the beautiful and marvelous interiors of the Spanish and Mexican cathedrals inspired them, and these Franciscans, unskilled as they were, sincerely tried to beautify their churches with the extremely limited means at hand. Most of the decorations are rather crude, not so much because the padres lacked taste, but because of the very situation confronting them. G. W. James wrote in his *In and Out of the Old Missions of California:*

> The great distance in this case between the desire and the performance is what makes the result pathetic. Instead of trusting to themselves,

or reverting to first principles as they did in architecture, the missionaries endeavored to reproduce from memory the ornaments with which they had been familiar in their early days in Spain . . . [they had] neither exactitude nor artistic qualities to fit them for their task.[29]

As to the criticism of the crudity and "primitivism," and the rather gaudy character of much of the painting at Santa Barbara Mission and elsewhere, a letter written to Mr. James by Fathers Glauber and Zephyrin will be of interest:

I do not think your criticism from an artistic view is too severe; but it would have been more just to judge the decorations as you would the efforts of amateurs, and then to have made sure as to their authors.

You assume that they were produced by the Padres themselves. This is hardly demonstrable. They probably gave directions, and some of them, in their efforts to make things plain to the crude mind of the Indians, may have tried their hands at work to which they were not trained any more than clerical candidates or university students are at the present time; but it is too much to assume that those decorations give evidence even of the taste of the Fathers. In that matter, as in everything else that was not contrary to faith or morals, they adapted themselves to the taste of their wards, or very likely too, to the humor

Fig. 25.   FACADE AFTER THE EARTHQUAKE IN 1925

Fig. 26. THE MISSION IN THE 1940's

of such stray "artists" as might happen upon the coast, or whom they might be able to import. You must bear in mind that in all California down to 1854, there were no lay-brothers accompanying the Fathers to perform such work as is done by our lay-brothers now, who can very well compete with the best of secular artists. . . . Hence the Fathers were left to their own wits in giving general directions, and to the taste of white "artists," and allowed even the Indians to suit themselves. . . . The Indians loved the gaudy, loud, grotesque, and as it was the main thing for the Fathers to gain the Indians in any lawful way possible, the taste of the latter was paramount.

     . . . the missionaries . . . after all did not put up these buildings and then decorate as they did for the benefit of future critics, but for the instruction and pleasure of the natives. . . .[30]

The mission fathers found that the California Indians had progressed only slightly beyond their prehistoric ancestors in the matter of artistic achievement and development. These Indians had a primitive knowledge of color, using only black, white, red from ochres, yellow, and green. They had no knowledge of binders such as oils. The Indians of Mexico were in this as in many other respects far more advanced. The artistic performance of the Indians, being extremely limited, was perhaps best expressed in their basketry and in their stone carving, their oldest art expression. Hence the wisdom and discretion of the padres was of great importance when the Indians were called upon to perform tasks for which they were unprepared.

Thus the introduction of primitive symbols such as the "River of Life," the double parallel lines representing serpents, and the sun, was the expression of individual taste. There is excellent expression of just such individualism in Santa Barbara Mission and at Santa Ines. The same was true of Teófilo, the neophyte painter of San Juan Capistrano who refused the conventional designs of the padres in his work. Quite often foreigners were hired to assist the padres in decorating; this was particularly true after the year 1800 when foreign ships stopped along the coast. The altar, and possibly much if not all of the Reredos at San Juan Bautista was painted by a Boston sailor named Thomas Doak. San Miguel's church was decorated by one Don Esteban Munras of Monterey, with Indians assisting. Santa Clara's third church was painted by Agustín Dávila, who used a very considerable amount of red derived from the cinnabar obtained at the nearby New Almaden mines.

Fig. 27.   SANCTUARY OF THE CHURCH IN 1953

Frequently the Indians, accustomed as they had been to execute the most primitive of pictographs, were allowed to express themselves in religious paintings. Generally the color schemes of these paintings was of the simplest: white, black, red, green, and blue. Often the pigments used in these paintings were those used in "fresco" work and hence contained no oils. The Indians had obtained their colors as natural pigments from the hills. Yellow ochre, sometimes exceptionally pure, was very common. White was obtained from the diatomaceous earth or from chalk; black from wood or bone charcoal or perhaps soot. Red was derived from cinnabar (a mercury ore) or from the red ochre in the hills. What blue there was came from bluish clays. It was quite natural for them to continue using their traditional colors in working in the churches.[31]

Not infrequently original elements of design were introduced—elements that, though primitive, were of an original and naturally aesthetic quality. The Indians understood this new phase of art for it lifted them to a higher plane than the one with which they had long been familiar. All the murals (in one sense "frescoes") were painted by the Indians under the direction of the padres. They had been often praised for their craftsmanship in pottery, basketry, wood, and stone work by Crespí, Font, Portolá, and Fages. That they could easily learn the techniques of brush work for painting and also stencil work was self-evident. This they learned from the above-mentioned decorators hired by the padres, or from the padres themselves. They were allowed especially to work on the walls of the *asistencia* chapels, of which an excellent instance was Pala. The earliest known decorated church was the one at Santa Clara, which had walls covered with whitewash and painted designs on the sanctuary walls. Vancouver commented on its good decoration.

Stencils were commonly used in covering large areas of wall. The designs at Santa Ines clearly show their use, for the wallpaper effect must have been achieved by that means. The stencils were probably cut from rawhide or leather. For the painting, shipments of colors and brushes for their application from Mexico were common. In the *memorias* of the Santa Barbara archives there are lists of paints requested by the padres between 1797 and 1809. The reds include *almagre* (a red ochre), *vermellón* (vermilion), orange, indigo (which was also used as a dye), *cardenillo* (a verdigris green), and purple or violet "ochre," as well as blues made from copper compounds, these in addition to the colors which were used by the natives.

Some of the original work on the walls at Santa Barbara endured until 1925, particularly in the running borders of fruit and flowers. The remaining designs and areas even before the complete restoration of 1926-1927 were "restorations" of earlier Indian work. Mary G. Holway [32] mentions that in 1920 there were:

Fig. 28.   RECONSTRUCTION OF THE FACADE AND TOWERS, 1952

. . . brilliantly colored rosetted figures from cedar on the ceiling . . . restoration[s] of the original designs made by the Indians representing the winged lightning. Within the chancel . . . also elaborate and vivid, appears the favorite All-seeing Eye radiating beams of light. . . .

At Santa Barbara, the paintings of undoubted Spanish origin are full of unusual interest; two lunettes in oil . . . and the Last Judgment (a copy of the canvas at the Escurial in Spain), are within the chancel . . . . The Descent From the Cross on the right wall near the altar and [to] the large painting of the Savior on the left. The curved shape of the lunettes would indicate that originally they were intended for placement directly over doors or windows or within an arch space. Their present position on flat walls as well as their technique is clear evidence of a foreign gift. High on the right wall over the arch spanning the recess containing the altar of the *Mater Dolorosa*[33] is a very large oblong painting of Hell, and above the arch directly opposite over the altar of St. Francis is a canvas of the same shape and size picturing Purgatory. The former is reminiscent of the theme as portrayed at Carmel . . . and described by Laperouse as he saw it there in 1786. In the scattering of the secularization period may not the canvas have found its way with the Purgatory to Santa Barbara, or may it not have been a gift from the generous Carmelo to one of the poorer mission chapels (San Miguel) which now possesses a work of the same motif? The canvas has disappeared from Carmel. Laperouse mentions also a companion picture representing Heaven, but it would seem a stretch of the imagination in connecting the Purgatory, even if dim, with that work. . . . However the two Santa Barbara paintings may have been direct gifts from Spain through Mexico. In Palou's list of church equipment brought north with the expedition to found California missions, mention is made of "eleven pictures of the Virgin" but of no other paintings. . . .

Two other large paintings of the same oblong shape and very dim, are equally interesting as those mentioned. Hung much lower than the Purgatory and beyond on the same wall, is a very ancient painting of three male figures which entirely fill the canvas, without background or detail to form an atmosphere.[34] On the right wall corresponding to this is a representation of three female saints, the central figure holding a vessel resembling a monstrance; the one of the left, the child in her arms, the Virgin Mother, and the one on the right with her foot on a skull holding a crucifix, evidently the penitent Magdalene.[35] The paintings are very poor in color, lacking brilliancy; this fact and the crude composition places them in an early period of Spanish art. A beautiful copy of the Virgin of Guadalupe from Mexico, over a side altar, a fine Assumption after Murillo in the drawing of the Virgin and cherubs, and a Crucifixion are close to the chancel rails. . . .

Stylistically, the Santa Barbara Mission is a curious mixture of Spanish, Moorish, and native. In it, both exterior and interior, one finds ecclesiastical as well as pagan motifs. For their prime source of design or motifs, applicable not only to the "decoration" but to the architecture itself, was the aforementioned copy of the long standard work on classical architecture, Vitruvius' *De Architectura*. Thus, the three engaged columns on each side of the front entrance are classical, Roman in origin; the triangular pediment between the towers is Greek; the curved and pointed arch of the spayed interior opening of the windows is a combination of Moorish and Roman arches; the wood carvings and designs on the ceiling are pagan motifs, and winged lightning and the thunderbird are Vitruvian and Indian respectively. But the entire approach to the problem is distinctly original and indigenous. Like many of the other Missions, it was its own style; the long narrow nave was the result of the limitations of the materials used to cover the distance between the supporting walls; the distance a heavy wooden beam could span, and, in addition, support the heavy tile roof. The walls were thick, as much as eight feet in some cases, again because of the nature of the materials used as well as the limited facilities for construction or lack of professional engineering. Stone walls forty-two feet high were made so thick in order that they support not only their own weight, but part of the roof load as well. The entire character of these heavy, massive buildings, the sum total of all the parts, is distinctly Californian. It is neither Spanish nor Moorish nor Mexican. It should, in fact, be called Franciscan architecture.

On June 29, 1925, a violent earthquake again shook the Santa Barbara area and severely damaged the entire Mission building compound.[36] Repair was undertaken that same year and restoration was completed in 1927. In that "restoration" considerable changes were made, a number of which have already been noted. A permanent altar of stone was installed and the floor level changed. The entire interior decoration, substantially the same at the present as it was twenty-five years ago, is, however, much more sumptuous, elaborate, and sophisticated than the pre-1925 interior designs, and is in no sense a preservation of the Indian or early designs save in the "marbled" designs painted on the pilasters and the dado on the side walls. (Figures 20, 21.)

The interior walls are decorated with "murals" in the form of dados, pilasters, ornamental arches, and friezes. The dado is four and one-half feet wide, rising above a fourteen-inch band just above the floor. It is continuous around the church, interrupted only by the doors themselves, the two side chapels, and the principal entrance. The colors used are a mixture of greens, "burnt orange," and white in a presumed imitation of what was believed to be the padres' and the Indians' concept of marble, or what was more likely, porphyry.

The pilasters, of which there are five on each wall, divide the nave into six sections that end at the low sprung arch that spans the rear of the church under the choir loft. The largest section is the space in the sanctuary. The pilasters are also painted with a reddish brown and white mottling. These vertical members are presumably representing "slabs" of marble and are quite well executed. The base proper of each is three feet one inch, the full width of the supporting structural member; the actual painted base of the "column" is twenty-four and one-half inches wide at dado height. The column (pilaster) itself is nineteen and one-half inches wide and projects about six inches from the wall. The base panel of the pilaster has a leafy, very conventionalized garland of leaves with a seven petaled flower at the center.

The windows are odd in shape, some being rectangular on the outer thickness of the wall, about three and one-half feet wide and five feet high, expanding inward to about four by six and one-half feet. The top of the window frame is a characteristic reversing curve or arc with an arch in the center. A rather elaborate and decorative garland of leaves and flowers with a small winged angel's head at the top follows the outline of the top arch of the window.

The doors are similarly treated. The large door leading to the cemetery is seven feet four inches wide inside the church; it narrows to five feet two inches at the actual door. The height inside is about eleven feet seven inches, with three ascending steps and the slight downward slope of the thickness of the wall overhead bringing the actual height of the door on the outside to seven feet ten inches. The opening is rectangular; that inside the church has a very low, sweeping reverse curve coming to a point above the center. It has a distinctly Moorish appearance. This "arch" is framed by two painted pilasters somewhat resembling Ionic columns, complete with capitals. Across and connecting them is a double lintel of painted marble. At each extremity is an ornament shaped like a pineapple or pine-cone; midway between is a decorative medallion, and connecting these a heavy garland. (Figures 18 and 19.)

The present Mission church now serves the Mission parish area. It is most solidly constructed, and since its restoration after the 1925 earthquake, the walls and ceilings have been reinforced with steel rods and other devices. The work of restoring rather than merely reconstructing the buildings was under the direction of the architect Ross Montgomery. The church proper is 175 feet long and 39 feet wide on the outside. The walls, varying in thickness, are approximately 6 feet thick and some 42 feet high, strengthened at intervals by heavy stone buttresses about 8 feet square and firmly anchored by means of steel plates to the walls. The double towers are 78 feet high and some 20 feet square. Though apparently solid stone masses, the south tower had in it a narrow spiral staircase leading up the bell platforms. In the base of the north tower is the baptistery, which is entered through a doorway inside the church near the front entrance. The roof is covered with tiles which were made by the Indians, most of them manufactured before 1825.

The nave of the church is 162½ feet long and 27½ feet wide. A door at the left rear corner of the Sanctuary, leading into the friary choir, has since 1925 been filled in. The triple door leading into the same room has been retained. High on the south wall of the Sanctuary is a "blind" window, the painted outline of what, in the earlier church was a true window. It is interesting that a similar device exists in the Sanctuary of Mission Santa Ines, but in that case, it is a false door. The two side chapels were for some years before 1925 barred by a high "wrought iron grille." The grille was removed and replaced with a low altar railing. The entrance from the sacristy into the Sanctuary is directly behind the main altar, which is about 5 feet in front of the Reredos wall. It cannot be seen from the front of the church.

In June, 1950, a second reconstruction of the Mission façade was begun. Unexplainable chemical deterioration of certain native materials used in the reconstruction of 1926 had caused deep cracks to appear in the base of each tower, and elsewhere on the façade. Upon demolition of the towers, the façade, and the steps, the native stone underlying the foundations was also found to be disintegrating. Completely new sub-foundations were poured and the towers reconstructed. The new towers are hollow. In the south tower, the old winding staircase was replaced by one placed against the inner walls, thus the steps serve as a series of internal buttresses. The north tower, with its baptistery in the base, was also changed. The original circular form with its domed ceiling had been retained in the 1926 restoration. The present baptistery is rectangular so as to reduce the mass-load on the foundation. The entire façade, including the steps, was rebuilt from the ground up. Although it is not identical with that previously used, the textural quality of the new facing stone is very attractive and more nearly resembles the original, to judge from paintings in the Mission collection.

The front area of the interior of the church was somewhat altered. A new entrance was made into the baptistery. The old (but not the original) confessionals were removed and new ones constructed; these are now immediately against the entrance wall. The choir area was also somewhat remodeled.

In July, 1953, the reconstruction of the Mission was completed and the rededication ceremonies took place on December 4 of the same year.

The present Mission building, with its unsurpassed background of mountains, and its resplendent church interior, is vastly different, and much more sophisticated in its decorative scheme than it was in the 1830's. Though the quality and the manner of decorating the interior walls was retained in both the 1926 and 1953 restorations, the style is very different. Perhaps it is more grand, more in the manner which the founding padres really desired. The strong pattern of the "marbleized" piers, and a few restored border patterns, are all that remain of the simple, though often crude and gaudy, but highly picturesque originals. Unfortunately, physical deterioration and the necessities of the contemporary life preclude an exact duplication—a true restoration of the building of the Mission of 1820.

MAP OF THE OLD MISSION BUILDINGS

This map was drawn up "from measurements taken with the assistance of the Padres by Samuel Newsom of the firm of Newsom and Newsom, Architects, San Francisco, August, 1905." It shows the extent of the buildings of that time and is of particular interest because the positions of the principal paintings and sculpture, as well as the chapels and side altars, are given by name, and their position in the church is specifically indicated.

The present sacristy at the rear of the church was, at that time, not yet constructed; but the "monks choir room" to the side was then divided into two unequal rooms, the smaller of which served as the vestment room. A notation in the corner states that this "small scale map taken from a drawing by Mr. Hawley [of] Santa Barbara."

The notations on the map indicate the location of the following: In the vestment room, an old crucifix in a case. In the Monk's choir room statues of St. Joseph and the Blessed Virgin Mary. In the sanc-

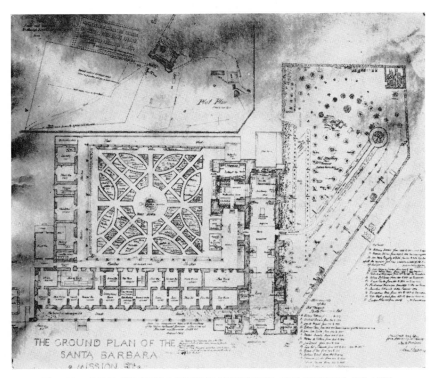

Fig. 29. MAP OF THE MISSION BUILDING COMPOUND IN 1901

tuary, on the Reredos wall: statue of St. Barbara in the center; "old Spanish statues of St. Anne and St. Joseph" on the east (epistle side); statues [sic] of St. Joachim and the Blessed Virgin on the west (gospel side). On the main altar, Faith, Hope and Charity. Over the door to the Monk's choir, the lunette The Last Judgment, 1793. (The date given refers possibly to its acquisition.) On the opposite wall Descent From the Cross picture. In the nave, at the foot of the steps to the sanctuary, was a small altar to St. Anthony on the south (left) side, and opposite, an altar to the Sacred Heart of Jesus. Next hung the large canvas, The Assumption of the Virgin (also given as 1793), also on the left. Continuing on this wall were, in order, an altar to St. Joseph, then one to St. Buonaventure [sic], then the painting of Purgatory and the "oratory" [sic] or recessed chapel with a statue of St. Francis according to Murillo. In the area beneath the choir were the "confession boxes." On the opposite (north) wall, was the recessed "oratory" with an altar and the statue of Our Lady of Sorrows. Next, the old painting of Hell, then an altar to St. Anthony, and next the large canvas of Jesus on Calvary (The Crucifixion).

At the time this map was drawn, there was no museum. Among other interesting notations is the complete and detailed listing of all the planting in and around the Mission gardens, and the adjoining cemetery; the names of those entombed in the mausoleum, and a list of all the "Missionaries of the Old Mission, Santa Barbara." Father Ludger Glauber was guardian at the time that the map was made. Further, of historic interest, is the exact designation and use of each of the rooms on the ground floor, from the carpenter's shop at the rear of the "west wing," to the Vicar General and Diocesan Administrator's room in the center of the long arcaded wing in the front.

This map, which exists as a faded photograph, measures 8⅝ by 7¼ inches, and is in the archives of the Mission Library.

Catalogue of
Paintings and Sculpture at
Mission Santa Barbara

Catalogue of Paintings and Sculpture at Mission Santa Barbara

The paintings of Santa Barbara Mission can be divided into religious works, secular (those important pieces not concerned with religious subject matter), and the "murals" (the wall, ceiling, and other decorations commonly found in all missions). The sculpture, almost without exception, is freestanding, and is all of a religious nature.

All of the works are numbered and follow a general pattern, beginning in the church proper for the first group, then in the foyer (*sala*) and the museum rooms open to the public. The remaining works are in the apartments, corridors, chapels, and choir of the Mission compound. Catalogue numbers preceded by the letter S refer to sculpture. Though some of the material has no direct bearing on the life of Santa Barbara Mission, it has, however, been included in the catalogue because of its importance and as examples of religious art of the Mission period, or of Spanish Colonial work, and also for its intrinsic value. Wherever possible the origin or source of the work described is given. The mention of the Mexican Invoices refers to the original assignment to the Mission; the Invoices were records of purchases, orders, or shipments of various goods and prepared usually in Mexico. Very frequently the work was not mentioned there but was otherwise recorded either in letters or accounts. Unfortunately definitive descriptions were not given. Inventories were presumably made every year, especially after 1832, but there are many gaps. They referred to the lists of objects or other properties in the possession of the Missions and prepared for the Mexican government. The earliest inventory date is 1835, and quite frequently certain works were for some reason or other not listed, or listed one year and omitted in another.*

Such an instance is noted in the Stations of the Cross, some of which are mentioned in several inventories and in others not at all, although it is obvious that all fourteen paintings were always together.

Where dimensions of works are given, the width precedes the height. If one dimension only is given, it indicates the height. All measures are in inches; they are rounded to the nearest whole figure.

Cat. No. S-1—Fig. 30.   GREAT CRUCIFIX ON THE REREDOS.
Polychromed wood. Life-size.

S-1. GREAT CRUCIFIX

Surmounting the entire Reredos and in the most prominent center position is a large polychromed wooden crucifix. It is set against a vividly painted burst of shafts of golden light. The dark brown wood of the cross effectively sets off the Corpus.

The hands are nailed, not to the ends of the cross bar, but about one-half way out. The figure is very nearly vertical, and there is not much curve of the weight of the body. It is entirely of one color, with little differentiation between the flesh tones and that of the loin cloth which, gathered somewhat to the left side, falls in folds almost to the knees. As is common in Spanish art, the wounds are realistically and very dramatically rendered. The gaping wound in the side has a dark stream of blood running down; the bruised knees and nail holes in both hands and feet are heavily stressed; the edges of the cross are also bloody. The wounds in the knees, elbows, and feet, as well as on the face and the shadows under the brows, are painted dark blue. The drops of blood from scratches on the face, chest and arms, and on the thighs are painted blue and dull red. The ribs are exposed through torn flesh on the back.

This is a simple, almost primitively direct Crucifix. The head is small; under the crown of thorns the blood shows, and again on the cloth. The chest and abdomen are treated very simply in flat planes in sharp contrast to the fussily gathered cloth that projects on the left in a most unnatural manner. The muscles of both arms and legs are correctly and directly treated. There is some agonizing strain in the nearly backward bend of the arms, whereas the legs are nearly relaxed and devoid of tension.

This great Crucifix contrasts markedly with the surrounding sculptures both in style and execution. However, the dramatic character is unfortunately lost because the Corpus, pale ivory in color, is virtually invisible against the light golden shafts that radiate from behind.

The figure is cracked almost its entire length from under the right arm, along the side, and down the leg.

This piece is not mentioned in any of the early reports. It is very likely of Mexican origin, dating probably from the mid-eighteenth century. It was not on the Reredos before the restoration of 1926, but was for many years in the friary choir just off the sanctuary. When the Reredos was reconstructed it was placed in its present position at the request of the then superior, Father Augustine Hobrecht, O.F.M.

S-2. ST. BARBARA

This is the largest figure on the Reredos, almost in the direct center below the large Crucifix. It is a typically Mexican Baroque polychromed wood figure with a somewhat theatrical quality. The characteristically expressionless face, its oval shape, indicates that it is a mid-eighteenth-century work. Yet it possesses some of the qualities of the extravagant seventeenth-century Baroque. Tradition and custom were so strong in Mexico that in some areas, or in some "schools," a conservatism obtained which resulted in a continued production of both sculpture and painting of an earlier period. The St. Barbara lacks the twisting, almost dancer-like pose of most Baroque statues; her pose and reserved expression are more neo-classical. But the sumptuous robes and the rich coloring are in the earlier tradition. It is a representative example of the fusion of styles in provincial Mexican sculpture.[1]

The saint wears a light blue, silvery "armor" over a long, dark blue-green robe; around her is wrapped a rather gaudy red over-dress with black and gold designs and a border in gold, and from the shoulders hangs an enveloping cape of the same material. One sleeve of the tunic shows; it is shell pink. She carries in her extended right hand a large silver ostensorium, and in her left a silver staff that ends in a palm frond. Her weight is on her left foot, thrusting the body over and forcing a turn and head slant that gives movement to the figure; she gazes intently at the Host in her hand. Her dark hair is simply drawn back. There is a thin golden nimbus around her head.

The statue is in very good condition, with the *estofado* retaining much of its original brilliance.

This statue is mentioned in the Mexican invoice dated February 6, 1793. Apparently this figure is one of the oldest pieces either of sculpture or painting belonging to the Mission. It is again mentioned in the Mission invoices of 1835, 1856, and 1858.

St. Barbara, or Santa Barbara, was martyred December 4, 303, A.D. She was the daughter of one Dioscorus who lived in the southeastern Roman empire at Heliopolis, a town not far from Memphis, Egypt. She was shut up in a tower by her father to protect her from suitors; during this time she secretly became converted to Christianity. Upon her father's discovery of her faith, he attempted to kill her,

Cat. No. S-2—Fig. 31.   ST. BARBARA ON THE REREDOS.
Polychromed wood. Life-size.

but she was borne away to safety by angels. Eventually she was
discovered, was tortured to force her to give up her faith, her father
himself finally beheading her. St. Barbara is the patron saint of fortifications, firearms, gunsmiths, and armorers. Her principal attribute
is a three-windowed tower. Quite frequently, she holds the Book, the
palm (a universal symbol of martyrdom), and often a sword.

S-3. THE IMMACULATE CONCEPTION

This statue of The Blessed Virgin Mary stands on a small projecting pedestal against a painted niche, at the left of center, some
twelve to fourteen feet above the floor of the Sanctuary. The figure
stands very nearly erect, the hands together as in prayer, the head

slightly turned to the right and looking almost down. The Virgin is dressed in splendid robes; her gown, with narrow cuffs on long sleeves, is golden with bright red. There is a clear, silvery, cobalt blue cloak with a red lining gathered on her left shoulder that comes across in front of her body at the waist, an effect which gives to the figure a feeling of motion. The face is simply and tastefully treated; there is no hint of dramatics or sentimentalism; the figure has a reserved beauty and a dignity. The dark brown hair is drawn away from the face. She wears a magnificent, heavy, silver crown about eight inches high, and the entire effect is one of richness and sumptuous beauty. Of heavy polychromed wood, it is Mexican in origin, and of the same style as the St. Barbara.

This statue has been in the Mission since December 31, 1795, and is listed as a statue of the Immaculate Conception, the silver

Cat. No. S-3—Fig. 32.   THE IMMACULATE CONCEPTION.
Polychromed wood. 48″.

crown being acquired in 1802. However, the absence of the conventional crescent, which is generally an integral and necessary part of the "Conception," and the fact that the figure is crowned, would indicate that this should now more correctly be titled The Blessed Virgin Mary as Queen of Heaven. In a photograph taken between 1874 and 1883, this same figure is standing on a crescent, but in all later photographs this crescent is absent. It is mentioned in the inventories of the Mission of 1835, 1855, and 1858.

S-4. ST. FRANCIS

Immediately below the Blessed Virgin Mary, on a small bracket, and against a classically draped painted niche, is a very fine statue of St. Francis. In his right hand he holds a Crucifix; his left is slightly raised. His somewhat bowed head is framed in a nimbus in the shape of radiating golden bursts of light.

The figure is very simply and directly carved from wood, and polychromed with a minimum of detail. It is one of the finest and most sensitively beautiful figures in any of the missions. The almost classical simplicity of the features and the absence of theatricalism, suggests a possible late seventeenth-century Spanish or Mexican origin.

The head is tonsured, and he wears a short beard, very dark in color. The expression of the face, especially in the eyes, is remarkable in its contemplation and inward vision. From this type of expression it was but a short step to the cloying sentimentality of later works. He wears a brown robe which, though subdued, reveals a fine gold and brown *estofado* pattern. This slightly patterned robe, with its rich tones, is an example of the license taken by the sculptor, for the plain grey of the traditional habit would have been too uninteresting on a sculptured piece. One can find considerable variety in the color of the Franciscan habit in the arts, especially in paintings. Originally the habit was of undyed wools that produced a grey color, and by 1260 this became standard. For years the Franciscans were known as the grey friars, and in early paintings (as by Giotto), they are represented in grey. At later periods other colors, principally blue, or blue-black, and sometimes black, were used. The St. Anthony in Figure 120, for example, is in dark blue; the St. Francis in Figure 93 is in a grey-and-white habit. This change in color was not so much the effect of artistic license on the part of the painters, but was due to the fact that the prescribed materials were often difficult to procure. Many paintings from Spain and Flanders show the Franciscans in blue or blue-grey; these date generally from the seventeenth century. The brownish color first appeared toward the end of the seventeenth century. The one identifying element in the habit which has remained constant is the knotted cord. Not until 1897, through a decree issued by Pope Leo XIII was the dark brown color made universal for the Franciscan habit.[2]

The statue has been broken in several places; the right arm at the shoulder and wrist, the left arm at the wrist, and all of the fingers of the left hand. Several of the fingers of the right hand have been restored.

This statue is first mentioned in the Mexican invoice of February 12, 1801, and in the Mission inventory of December 31, 1801, indicating that it had arrived in the interval at the Mission. It is subsequently mentioned in the inventories of 1835, 1855, and 1858.

St. Francis, the founder of the Franciscans, is one of the best loved and most frequently presented saints in ecclesiastical art. He was born in the Italian town of Assisi in 1182, and after an early life given over to worldliness, dedicated himself to a religious life at the age of twenty-five. He became a wonderful preacher and drew to himself many converts. His Order, having poverty, chastity, and obedience as its principal vows, was approved by Pope Innocent III in 1209; his disciples were called the "Friars Minor," or "Lesser Brothers," to signify that humility should be their chief attribute.

Francis is represented principally as a man of great kindness and understanding of all living things. His common attributes, besides the robe with its cowl and the three knotted cord used as a belt, are the stigmata, the lamb which he carried, and the birds. He died October 4, 1226, and was canonized two years later.

S-5. ST. JOSEPH

On the right of St. Barbara is the nearly life-size sculpture of St. Joseph carrying the Infant Jesus in his left arm. He is dressed in a garish and very Baroque costume, principally black with elaborate golden designs of leaves and stems, and the outer mantle principally yellow with gold, bright red, and dark blue flowers painted on it. From the left shoulder hangs a red-lined cloak.

The Infant Jesus is a small, separately carved figure clothed in white satin, a most incongruous feature, yet one which remains char-

Cat. No. S-4—Fig. 33. ST. FRANCIS. Polychromed wood. 30″.

Cat. No. S-5—Fig. 34.   ST. JOSEPH.   Polychromed wood.   48".

acteristic of the eighteenth century customs, and particularly of Colonial Spanish sculpture.

Joseph's right hand is extended forward; the thumb and middle fingers almost touching, holding the traditional lily-flowered staff.

This polychromed wood statue is very simply carved; the head, with a dark moustache and beard, and close-cropped dark hair, is encircled by a large, thin, circular nimbus. For all its "over-dressed" character and its inconsistencies that very nearly make it amusing in its approach, it is a fine and impressive work. It is similar in style and manner, and is probably from the same "school" as the St. Barbara and the Conception.

The exact date of the arrival at the Mission of this statue is not known, but it is first mentioned in the inventory of December 31, 1795, and then again in those for the years 1835, 1855, 1856, and 1858.

S-6. ST. DOMINIC

One of the most beautiful of the sculptures on the Reredos is the one of St. Dominic in the lower right-hand corner. Like the St. Francis opposite, it is about thirty inches high.

Cat. No. S-6—Fig. 35.   ST. DOMINIC.   Polychromed wood.   30".

The saint stands erect, looking directly before him, his wide cowl open at the throat, effectively framing a small head set upon a very slender neck; his two hands extend before him, holding a long rosary. Under the heavy dark cloak, which is gathered into "classical folds" under his right arm and gathered into the crook of his left, is his full white habit over which is a scapular.

His face is almost mask-like. It is bearded, and the hair, close-cropped, is like a close fitting nimbus. The metal halo, affixed to the back of the head, was long missing and has been only recently found.

The wooden sculpture is riddled with worm holes and chipped here and there; and all the fingers of the right hand have been broken off. It is a characteristic classical work, with very subdued *estofado;* save for the realistic pallor and color of the face and lips, white, black, and gold are the only colors used. It is probably from the same period as the St. Francis.

This statue was sent from Mexico on March 18, 1806; its date of arrival is unknown. It is mentioned in the Mission inventory of 1835, 1855, and 1858.

St. Dominic, confessor and founder of the Order of Preachers commonly known as the Dominican Order, was born of noble descent in Castile and died in Bologna in August, 1221. In 1184 he entered the University of Palencia, where he studied for ten years. In 1203, he first conceived of founding an Order for the purpose of combating heresy, especially the Albigensian heresy. He taught and preached throughout Europe. Dominic bound his friars to corporate poverty (modified in 1475) and to the monastic laws of silence, fasting, office in choir, common life, and the three vows. The Order was founded in 1216, and two years later he founded the Order of Dominican nuns. He was canonized by Gregory IX on July 13, 1234, and his feast day is August 4. Though he did not originate the Rosary, he popularized its use. His attributes are a dog at his side, the star on or above his head, and a lily in one hand, a book in the other.

S-7. THE BISHOP'S TOMB

Though not exactly a work of sculpture, the tomb is nonetheless interesting for its simple relief with characteristically painted details. It is on the right wall of the church, on the Epistle side of the Altar, and at right angles to the Reredos, which it adjoins. It is five feet three inches wide, and seven feet ten inches in height at the corner.

The central medallion is a painting representing the Blessed Mother with the Christ Child as Our Lady of Refuge. The border is rather crudely lettered (painted) "F. Franciscus Garcia Diego Prim. Epis. Californ."

The entire "façade" is of wood painted to represent marble. Below the medallion, in a rectangular plaque, is the bishop's obituary. The capitals of the smooth semi-engaged pillars are carved in imitation of Ionic volutes. The "pillars," "architrave," and "cornice" are in pinkish tone and color, as is the obituary plaque. The "pediment" is light blue, the principal area is blue-green; the area surrounding the medallion is painted to imitation of green marble or porphyry, as is the base.

The bishop's miter, and the Host and chalice beneath it are in wood relief; the miter has a design painted on it. This tomb was made shortly after the bishop's death in 1846, and was undoubtedly designed by the same person who had planned the elaborate high altar for the bishop. The painting in the medallion is identical with that which surmounts the altar. (See Figure 130.)

All details, as well as the total concept of the tomb indicate the influence of the neo-classic movement in both sculpture and architecture. Such "tombs" are very similar to the *entradas* and niches designed by the Mexican architect Francisco Eduardo de Tresguerras (1759-1833), whose principal center of activity was at Celaya. The main church in Aguas Calientes, Mexico, in the strict neo-classical style of Tresguerras was completed in 1841 for Bishop García Diego. This was shortly before the bishop came to California, and it is reasonable to assume that he would have planned for a cathedral in the "modern" style of the period, and that his tomb would be along the same lines.

The Most Reverend Francisco García Diego y Moreno, the first Bishop of California, was appointed Bishop of both Californias on April 27, 1840. He was familiar with California missions, having been stationed at Mission Santa Clara from 1833 to 1835. In December, 1840, Santa Barbara was selected as the seat of the Episcopal See, and plans were made for the construction of the Cathedral together with a theological school and seminary, as well as a palace. The condition of affairs at that time, both political and economic, made it impossible to realize these plans, and Bishop Diego was forced to request permission from Governor Alvarado to take up residence at the Mission. The Bishop possessed no other residence in California. He found the situation at Santa Barbara too crowded, and through Fathers Jimeno and Moreno at Mission Santa Ines, petitioned the new governor, Micheltorena, for a grant of land within the Santa Ines territory.[3] Six square leagues (some 36,000 acres) of land, plus an annual stipend of $500.00 were granted for the seminary in 1845. Thus the first educational institution in California was founded by the Bishop, and it was given the name of The College of Our Lady of Refuge of Sinners. Later, when the "College" was established, the name was changed to the Seminary and College of Our Lady of Guadalupe, in 1854. The school endured until 1881.

Bishop García died April 30, 1846, and the funeral took place on May 3. It was in accordance with his wishes that he was not buried in the vault beneath the Sanctuary, but in the especially prepared tomb on the Epistle side of the Altar.

Cat. No. S-7—
Fig. 36.   THE BISHOP'S TOMB.
Wood and plaster.

Cat. No. S-8—
Fig. 37.   HIGH ALTAR CRUCIFIX.
Polychromed wood.   19x34 (corpus 16x17).

S-8. HIGH ALTAR CRUCIFIX

There is a wide variety of Crucifixes in the Mission, ranging in size from the majestic Reredos figure to small, rather delicate works. This Crucifix, although following the general pattern as to style, is a combination of style characteristics. In contrast to the necessarily broader treatment of the great Reredos figure, this is more sensitive and in one sense, more emotional in feeling.

The work is consistent with the later Baroque type-sculpture and carving of mid-eighteenth-century Mexico. Though it lacks the more extravagant twisting and turning of the more theatrical Crucifixes of the period, some of these qualities are retained, as for example, the treatment of the elaborately gathered and tied loin cloth. There is only slight movement in the line of the body, and that is realized in the manner of crossing the feet. In fact, the figure—somewhat restored—is more in the tradition of the seventeenth-century classical Spanish style than of the Mexican Baroque. The figure of Christ is realized here rather as a superb, beautiful figure of very nearly ideal proportions, and the body is virtually unblemished, in direct contrast to the unrestrained and often brutal expression that is more in the tradition of Mexican or Spanish emotionalism.

The Christ is represented here on the Cross before death, and though His body hangs from the arms of the Cross, there is little feeling of sagging weight. On the contrary, the very position of the extended and upraised arms and the slight drooping of the head suggest (perhaps this may have been intentional), the coming Resurrection, for there can be visualized both the Ascension and the gesture of universal compassion and blessing in this pose.

Although the figure has been restored—it had at one time been broken at the shoulders and the thighs—it retains its original color quality. There is a monochrome character in the near ivory-white of the *encarnación,* which, however, has been somewhat destroyed and obscured by a later repainting. The hair and beard are a warm brown color; the few bruises and the wound in the side are a dull red. The eyes, which are deeply set in overhanging brows, are partially open, and are made of porcelain. The result is a restrained emotionalism. The crown of thorns is made of woven cord.

The figure is principally of carved wood, with gesso for minor details, while the loin cloth is a combination of wood carving, gesso-dipped cloth, and gesso. The cross to which the Corpus is attached is of rusticated wood and is of a considerably later date.

S-9. SANCTUARY LAMP

Though this old sanctuary lamp no longer hangs in the Mission church, it is an interesting example of this type of Mexican work. The lamp had been in long usage before it was replaced by the larger one during the 1880's. At some later date, a large dark red glass for holding the candle replaced, or rather, was substituted for the reservoir of oil.

The lamp is made in two parts, partly of silvered tin and of brass with a silver overlay or plating. It is a cast piece made probably in imitation of the heavy silver pieces that hung in Mexican churches. Proportions and design are pleasing in the neo-classical ornamental style prevalent in the early nineteenth century. The sides are fluted and medallioned, with two plain areas and one of formalized acanthus leaves. The three angel heads with wings are of cast brass, gilded and riveted to the bowl. To them are attached the brass chains for hanging the lamp. The original thin silver plating is gone from the cover or top part of the bowl; this part is now a dull brass color, which may indicate, however, that the two parts do not belong to each other.

The workmanship throughout is excellent and a fine indication of the attention paid to detail in the manufacture of church goods.

Cat. No. S-9—
Fig. 38.   OLD SANCTUARY LAMP.
Silver-plated brass. 9x9.

Cat. No. 10—
Fig. 39. OUR LADY OF SORROWS.
Oil on canvas. 27x35.

10. OUR LADY OF SORROWS

This work is a three-quarter-length figure painting of Our Lady executed almost entirely in varying intensities and shades of blue, with the tunic and scarf in grey. It is a painting characteristic of the late eighteenth century, of one of the Mexican schools, yet having traces of seventeenth-century Spanish in the expression, somewhat in the style of Morales. The face, a long oval, is turned upward. The expression is not particularly successful, and is just short of being vapid. It is well modeled, and the flesh tones are good. There is a faint suggestion of an aureole.

The left hand is held at the breast, from which point radiate seven "swords" (the seven dolors), four on her right, three on her left. The handles are gold in color. The right hand is extended downward, palm turned up, almost in the corner of the canvas. The pose is similar to that of the Mary in the large Crucifixion. (Figure 63.) This particular pose is characteristic of many Mexican works. There is in the "museum" at Guadalupe-Zacatecas (Mexico) a large Crucifixion by Miguel Herrera, active in Mexico City during the last third of the eighteenth century. This painting is far superior in drawing, color, and general execution to either of the Santa Barbara works, and may possibly have been the prototype. Herrera's work is softer and the participants at Calvary seem almost to be members of a poetic drama.

The *Dolorosa* is an example of a characteristic type of devotional painting so common in both Spanish and Mexican art, the type of painting appealing to the emotionalism of the Latins of that period, but artistically it is rather an inferior work. The painting is in very poor condition; the canvas has been remounted by having been glued to a cloth which was tacked to the stretcher.

The painting arrived at the Mission between 1866 and 1868.

The *Mater Dolorosa,* or Lady of Sorrows, or Sorrowful Mother, is commonly represented in sculpture with one dagger piercing her heart. In painting, however, she is very frequently shown with seven swords; these represent the devotion of the seven dolors: the prophecy of Simon, the Filght to Egypt, the loss of the Child Jesus at Jerusalem, meeting Jesus on the road to Calvary, and the Burial. Hence representations are also called Our Lady of Seven Dolors. The devotion was first granted to the Servite Order in 1668.

11. THE ASSUMPTION AND CORONATION OF THE VIRGIN

This painting, a large composition from the "Murillo" school, is one of the two largest canvases at the Mission. The dominant and central figure is the conventional Mary, here very young, sweetly resigned, head bowed and slightly turned away from center. The hands are crossed at the breast; the standing pose is as relaxed as though

Cat. No. 11—Fig. 40.   ASSUMPTION AND CORONATION OF THE VIRGIN.
Oil on canvas. 103x168.

she were about to kneel. Her robe is white, the mantle is clear blue, and is the strongest color in the canvas. The warm, brown hair is loose around the head and falling to the shoulders. There is a grey-gold, filmy scarf between the cloak and the throat. She stands on clouds, and at her feet are the protruding heads of three cherubs. These are well painted but are lacking in much expression. The figure is about life size, simply done, and not too sweet.

Behind and above the Virgin Mary are the three figures of the Holy Trinity, all three clothed in white and seated on clouds. In the center, looking directly down upon the head of Mary before Him, is God the Father. He holds the golden, arched crown in both hands. To the left and a bit lower is the Son, in face and expression very like the Father. His left hand is extended, palm upward, almost to the crown. To the right is the personification of the Holy Ghost. This figure balances the Son; the head, likewise inclined toward Mary, is by far the best and most "spiritual" of the three. At the feet of this figure are the heads of three cupids emerging from clouds. Each of the heads has fine rays of light emanating from behind them.

Almost a dominating figure, to the detriment of the composition, is the large cross-bearing angel in the lower left corner. Though clad in a blue-green-grey tunic that almost merges into the cloud-sky background, its life size and the strong light on the face and arm detract from the central figure. The angel wears a red scarf; the wings are dark grey-brown. The head and face are well painted but the expression is rather vapid: the face, upturned, looks into space away from the center, the eyes are full, limpid and rolled upward, the mouth partly open, a characteristic, baroque, allegorical figure derived from the Flemish (Rubens) rather than the Spanish school.

Opposite is another angel, younger. This figure is almost an anachronism in that it is plump, fleshy, and far more earthy in character than it is spiritual. In each upper segment, above, and to the right and left of the Trinity, are groups of three child angels emerging from clouds.

The painting appears to be unfinished in several parts. Most conspicuous is the bottom section between the two angels, especially toward the right of the canvas where a yellowish "light" or cloud surrounds the figure, but which area terminates abruptly against the dark blue. Likewise, certain details of the large angels' wings are indicated; the sandal straps are vermillion lines with no shading to follow the modeled form of the feet (this could, of course, be a later addition). It appears to be, however, a development in the under-painting and a ground for the composition.

Another point suggesting incompleteness is the irregularity of the vaporous light quality that is found here and there in the work. This is a good example of the religious painting of the eighteenth century in Mexico, and, as is often the case, may represent the work of several painters, a common practice in studios and schools, especially when commissions of this type were executed. It is quite possibly a work from the Mexican studio of Miguel Cabrera.[4]

In the former convent of Guadalupe, Zacatecas, there are a number of canvases in which there are representations of the Holy Trinity. One, which is by Cabrera, has almost the identical poses and facial proportions of the Santa Barbara painting. Still other paintings of the Trinity, again with strong resemblances in proportion, expression, and coloring, are the known works of Cabrera pupils and followers. One of his students, Juan de Saenz, was painter of a Trinity that is apparently a derivation of the above-mentioned Cabrera. Either could have worked on the Santa Barbara canvas. The similarities, especially of the Trinity, appear in other paintings in the Mission; see Figure 108 and (to a lesser extent) Figure 102. The rather conventional or manneristic treatment of the Trinity with the curiously pointed oval faces, the very small mouths, and the slight inclination of the heads, appears in virtually all later Mexican paintings representing this subject. By the end of the eighteenth century this became a stereotype.

The painting was not specifically mentioned until the inventory of 1835, and then again in 1858. It was, however, brought to the Mission in 1798.

Since the middle of the eighteenth century the Holy Office has decreed that the Holy Spirit may not be represented in human form either with the Father and the Son, or separately. Pope Benedict XIV made this prohibition in an epistle entitled *Sollicitudini* dated October 1, 1745. Specifically, it prohibited depicting the Blessed Trinity as one body with three heads, or three separate persons. The Canon (1279) was subsequently again approved, confirmed, and ordered published by Pius XI on March 16, 1928. Allowing for the considerable lapse of time for promulgations and laws to be circulated, the presence of the Trinity as in this painting makes possible the dating of the work as about the middle of the century. On the other hand, edicts and laws of the Church, especially in Mexico, were often completely ignored when it came to matters concerning the fine arts. On a few occasions, however, the Office of the Inquisition did interfere and caused changes to be made in paintings.

S-12. CRUCIFIX: SIDE ALTAR

This small Crucifix on the side altar near the Sanctuary is possibly a seventeenth-century Spanish work. It is a small, finely executed piece, which shows a strong retention of the late Gothic style. The Cross, which is not squared, is in imitation of a rough tree, and may be a modern piece. It is very likely that the Corpus is a much older piece and was attached at some later date.

The Corpus is well carved, with considerable movement in the figure, yet withal retaining a primitive angularity. It is bowed out away from the Cross. The treatment is throughout very realistic; the ribs are extremely pronounced, but not correct in number. The neck is rather long, the head and face quite pointed and most sensitively

handled. The drapery at the loins is simply modeled. In the palms of the hands and at the feet are large pyramid-headed nails. The gaping wound in the right side has blood oozing, the knees are bruised, and there are other marks.

The *encarnación* of the figure is a light grey-white, with the hair and the beard a very dark brown, almost black. The fingers of the left hand are broken off. The fingers and parts of the head and the features were modeled in gesso before the finishing of the figure. It is a very good piece, sensitive without being sentimental.

Cat No. S-12—
Fig. 41. SIDE ALTAR CRUCIFIX.
Polychromed wood. 13x19 (corpus 9x12).

The Crucifix is not mentioned in the inventories, and there is no data on its accession. However, it may be one of the two Crucifixes "about 25 inches high" brought to the Mission in 1798.

THE FOURTEEN STATIONS OF THE CROSS

These fourteen paintings are done in oil on canvas and measure 24½ by 15¼. They are fairly uniform in character: the color, the generally low key, the somewhat stilted and often theatrical poses are similar throughout. Most of the compositions are flat; that is, there is little forward-backward movement, and for the most part, the figures in them are set on one plane against a background. In most instances, the fundamental plan of the compositions is excellent. They are painted simply and well; they lack, however, the quality of emotional expression which would lift them above the realm of factual illustration into the field of creative interpretation. However, the unknown artist who painted these was no mere illustrator, for he understood at least the value of dramatic contrasts, and also, for the most part, successfully made use of color balance, and he rarely sentimentalized his subject matter. There is an inconsistency in the drawing of very nearly every figure in the series; the proportions are unusual in that, for the head sizes, the figures are very short and stocky, having long bodies and short legs. In most instances, the heads appear too large for the bodies. Occasionally the articulation of the arms and legs is awkward and reveals the painter's lack of understanding the structure of the human figure, which, coupled with the curious expressions of some of the members of the drama, gives to these persons an air of self-consciousness.

What has saved all of these paintings, the entire series of the Stations, from degenerating into sentimental illustrations is their unconscious crudity of drawing. Fortunately, the incorrect drawing and lack of proportion in the majority of the paintings is clothed in the simple color harmony that ties each composition together. These are all the work of a sincere artist, a man who was not a master of the figure in movement, but who had a certain sense of color organization.

Again attribution of artist or school must be chanced. There is a set of Stations in the former convent at Guadalupe-Zacatecas painted by Gabriel Joseph de Ovalle in 1749, which have precisely the same quality in the drawing of the figures. The color of these, however, is much harder and brighter and the facial expressions are more intense. Other works by this painter at Guadalupe are much softer in tonality. Crude and awkward as the Santa Barbara Stations may be, the painter was quite skillful in his handling of color and in his brushwork.

The fourteen Stations were sent as a group from Mexico on April 20, 1797, and were at the Mission by December of that year.[5] They were then valued at 140 pesos. The only other mention of the Stations is in the inventory of 1858.

13. First Station: Jesus Is Condemned

This canvas is in very good condition although extremely dark. It is simply planned and quite symmetrical. There is arrested or incipient movement, despite the arrangement of the figures, which is rather stiff. The color is keyed very low; warm reds, orange, and yellow predominate on the right side, grey-green, green and blue on the left.

The central figure is Christ in a blue robe, with bared feet

Cat. No. 13—Fig. 42. FIRST STATION

and head bowed towards Pilate on the right. A soldier with a lance holds the rope which is tied around the neck of Christ. Behind the two is another figure; to the right of Christ stands a robed old man. The face of Christ is strongly illuminated and contrasts with the heavy dark brown of the crown of thorns. The eyes are cast down in resignation. Two disciples nearby have moderately concerned expressions.

The right half of the composition is dominated by Pilate in a blue tunic and sandals, with a blue cape and a vermillion cloak draped over his shoulders and across his lap. He sits on a raised chair and the steps to his seat are covered with an oriental rug, which ties together the colors of the composition. The right hand of Pilate is raised towards Christ; his face is turned down to the scribe as though dictating. He holds a thin staff in his left hand.

Between Pilate and Christ is a boy, similar to one of Murillo's urchins, with one hand on a water jug. In the corner near Pilate is the scribe clad in yellow with white sleeves and collar, about to write down the pronouncement. He is seated at a table covered in dark blue on which is an inkstand with quill pens and a sheet of paper. His face is bearded and he looks at Christ with a curious, dubious expression.

14. Second Station: Jesus Bears His Cross

The composition here is good, with effective contrast of the vertical lines of the building and arch and two soldiers at the left with the diagonal of Christ, the cross, and two men. Christ, clothed in blue, in the center, is moving toward the left, and is surrounded by the brown bodies of soldiers, and the heavy cross.

A bright orange-red banner in the upper left and spots on a soldier's tunic, also on the left, balance and intensify the grey cast of the remainder of the composition. The plastic movement is well handled, with the figure of the foreground soldier establishing deep space relationship between himself and Christ, and forcing the eye inward, while the background wall keeps the composition two dimensional. The light pattern is fair; the face and hand of Christ are sharply illuminated. There is also light on the shoulder, which moves along the arm, chest, and thigh of the man behind Christ.

This is a far better painting than the First Station. The expressions, however, are postured. The canvas is in good condition.

Cat. No. 14—Fig. 43.   SECOND STATION

Cat. No. 15—Fig. 44. THIRD STATION

15. Third Station: Jesus Falls the First Time

The composition is based almost entirely on diagonals forming a well-knit abstract design. The figure of Christ is in the center of the foreground; at the left are two soldiers with lances, and behind Christ, a man is bending to help Him up. In front of Christ, to the right, is a figure leaning and moving to the right with his head turned inward, thus organizing the composition and creating good movement.

There is good contrast of the slanted poses of the figures with the static verticals and horizontals of the buildings in the right background. The color distribution is also pleasing, the dominant tone being a silvery blue-grey, slightly greenish. The light grey of the tunic of Christ is further intensified by the dark blue of His cloak or mantle, a dark which effectively unifies the low key of the ground color. The only sharp color contrast is the red of the cloak of the armor-clad soldier at the extreme left.

The flesh tones are all a warm, golden brown, excepting for the unearthly, ivory-like pallor of the face and hands of Christ. The sky is grey-blue (originally perhaps, cobalt) with a light streaking of clouds.

Although this is a small canvas, it has the quality of bigness.

16. Fourth Station: Jesus Meets His Mother

The principal figure to the left of center is Christ, clad in grey-blue and blue, and bowed down with the cross. To the right of center is His sorrowing Mother, leaning forward, hands crossed on her breast. She is also entirely clad in blue. Between her and Christ is

Cat. No. 16—Fig. 45.   FOURTH STATION

a man in the background, helping with the cross. This figure, in a very low, brown key serves to set off the blue of the two principals and to create a symmetrical composition.

To the right of Mary and somewhat in the background are two figures (of disciples), one weeping, holding a cloth to his face, the other at the extreme right, about to move forward in compassion. Again is found the use of bright red-orange at the outer field of the composition. This group of four is balanced by three Roman soldiers behind Christ. One of them, in the middle, has a dull red-pink mantle; the one on the extreme left wears a red cap. The sky is dull blue, the earth a grey olive-brown. The faces of the Christ and of His mother and her hands are the only sharply contrasting values.

The composition is very static in spite of the inclination of the two figures towards the center. There is minor movement within the two groups, and some in the center. The heads of all of the eight figures are very nearly on a horizontal line. The drawing in this Station is quite weak, the heads of the principal figures being quite out of scale, and with expressions of sorrow and anguish that are stereotyped and not too well realized.

There is slight damage to this canvas, with holes in the lower right quarter, and small tears.

17. Fifth Station: Jesus is Relieved by Simon of Cyrene

This composition, for all its implied movement of figures, is essentially static. To the left of center is the bowed figure of Christ, with a taut rope about his neck, led by a Roman. An armored soldier at the right prods Him on. The movement out of the composition to the right is effectively stopped by this inward leaning figure. Immediately behind Christ is Simon, offering a silver coin to a Roman soldier.

This is one of the weakest of the compositions. In spite of there being only five figures, the effect is nonetheless crowded. The figures, especially the one leading Christ, are postured, the result of too great a concern with the literary features of the scene.

Cat. No. 17—Fig. 46. FIFTH STATION

The color is more lively than in the preceding station, and there is greater variability. The blue-grey-green tone pervades, with the dark brown of the cross and the ochre of the earth. Christ in the center is in blue, Simon in brown, and the soldier with him in yellow ochre and metallic grey. On the right the leading figure is grey with a reddish shirt, and brown shoulders and legs. The soldier at the right is in grey armor, blue breeches, tan kilt and leggings.

The canvas is slightly marred and is very dirty.

18. Sixth Station: Jesus Meets Veronica

This is one of the better compositions of the Stations, being built on opposing diagonals and sharp contrasts of color and value. The silhouettes against the typical blue sky form an irregular inverted triangle with the apex at the most important point, where Veronica wipes the brow of Christ. Christ and Veronica are enclosed in another triangle.

To the left is the figure of Simon, helping with the cross, and facing a standing Roman soldier who has his back to the spectator. This placing of the two figures in juxtaposition achieves a sort of three-dimensional space which moves back from the soldier to Simon,

Cat. No. 18—Fig. 47.   SIXTH STATION

forward to the extended bracing foot of Christ, somewhat back to Veronica, and forward again along her leg on the ground. Thus there is a forward-backward zigzag as well as a lateral one. The sharpest and most dramatic figure is the minor one who has led Christ by the rope. This figure counteracts with its diagonal axis the down-right movement of the principal triangle.

Attention to the principal figures is logically achieved by using the sharp, white vertical edge of Veronica's handkerchief, the upper end of which connects with the less intense effulgence about Christ's head. Christ, in blue, and blue-grey robe, opposes the rose-colored skirt and tan and grey of Veronica's robe. The red appears again in the scarf of the soldier and the rust red of Simon.

There is a curious gap, or tension, between the figures of Christ and of Veronica. The positions are extremely awkward, and the extended right arm of Christ to Veronica serves only to accentuate this gap. Yet, withal this awkwardness, it is a superior composition.

19. Seventh Station: Jesus Falls the Second Time

This composition, made up of five figures, has rather arrested movement. The stumbling figure of Christ in blue, is in the center, silhouetted in light against the dark mass of a building which towers

Cat. No. 19—Fig. 48. SEVENTH STATION

behind Him to fill in almost a third of the background. The almost invisible Cross is also against this mass. To the left is a slave, stripped to the waist, holding up the arm of the Cross, the line of his body and that of the cross forming the dominant triangle in which the bowed Christ moves. Behind and to the left, is a Roman in dark red, stooping to the ground, the curve of his body repeating somewhat the curve of the body of Christ. To the right of Christ is the man with the rope, leaning away from Him, as is the Roman soldier with the lance at the extreme right and more in the foreground. These two, with the slave, establish three parallel slanting lines to contrast with the two bowed figures and the sharp verticals of the buildings.

The painting is in a very low key. Here the most luminous spots are the highlights on the back, arm, and face of Christ, which are very sharply contrasted against His hair and beard. The colors are well balanced. Perhaps the red, tan, and blue of the soldier at the right is somewhat too insistent, but it does establish a plastic depth. The drawing of the fallen Christ is awkward, the artist having been unable to master the foreshortening of the arm and the turn of the body.

The canvas is in good condition.

20. Eighth Station: Jesus Meets the Women of Jerusalem

Of all the stations, this painting has the most sense of depth and space. The painter has attempted, with fair success, to give a feeling of depth and plastic modeling.

Christ stands almost erect in the direct center, His right hand extended to a woman kneeling before Him to the left. His left arm supports the arm of the Cross. Christ is flanked by a fully clothed man on His right, and on His left by a lance-bearing Centurion who stands easily, talking to another soldier at the extreme right of the canvas. There is another woman at the extreme left seated on the ground with an infant in her arms.

Behind the two women, and extending beyond Christ, is a landscape of rolling hills painted in browns and blue-greys. At the right is an archway through which the sky is visible.

There is much more movement, both plastically and laterally, than in most of the other Stations. The figures very nearly fill the area without crowding. However, the drawing is poorer here than in some of the others; an attempt at slight foreshortening of the body of Christ has resulted in an awkwardly drawn figure. The poses

are for the most part stiff and postured, and the face of the woman
with the infant is plainly sentimental rather than compassionate.

Christ, in blue, is almost lost in the surrounding low key of the
Cross and the two men. Even the pallor of the skin in much less
luminous than in the other canvases. The red and blue of the
Centurion's uniform at the extreme right is much more subdued than
it has been in the other Stations. The most conspicuous figure in
this composition is the kneeling woman in the foreground. Bareheaded,
with a light grey veil, her dress is a golden color, which is sharply
set off by the blue of her cloak or mantle. The flesh color of her face,
throat, and arms forms a small luminous triangle.

Cat. No. 20—Fig. 49. EIGHTH STATION

21. Ninth Station: Jesus Falls the Third Time

This composition, presenting the fall of Christ for the third time,
is in very dramatic contrast to the preceding and following Stations.
There is only the barest suggestion of a vertical line. Roughly, the
composition is elliptical, with arm and body direction producing a
strongly moving pattern. The movement is established by the curve
of the arm of the soldier at the rear who, with his right hand, tries
to stay the fall of the heavy Cross. The line extends to the right

Cat. No. 21—Fig. 50.   NINTH STATION

across his shoulder and to the head of the man on the extreme right, along this man's bare arm directly to the luminous hand and arm which frame the face of the fallen Christ. From here the movement extends along the leg of the soldier who is pushing Christ with his foot, up his thigh, back and upper arm, to meet the arm of the soldier in back. This circular motion is well braced by the diagonals of the spear at the back, the man on the right, and the nearly vertical legs of the two men to the left of Christ. The only true vertical is the axis of a leafy dark green tree at the extreme left of the canvas, and one at the extreme right. There is no architecture here, only the rolling hills, a rocky foreground, and a cloudy, streaked sky.

The color organization is good, with the blue-white of Christ's robe as the dramatic highlight in the center, repeated in the tunic of the man on the right who is creating tension by pulling at the rope tied about Our Lord's neck. This figure is badly drawn. The inevitable patches of red are here placed nearer to the center, the most luminous immediately above the head of Christ, the other very much subdued, to the left above a deep brown shadow. The dark brown diagonals of the heavy Cross, although almost lost in the low key of the shadows, effectively intensify the dramatic curves of the whole. This is one of the best of the Stations.

22. Tenth Station: Jesus is Deprived of Clothing

This composition is based almost entirely upon vertical lines, with five very nearly parallel figures contrasting effectively with one kneeling in the foreground. The painting shows Christ in the center being unclothed by the soldier at the left. Immediately to the right of Christ and behind Him is the man who holds the rope, his skin a very dark brown, contrasting effectively with the whiteness of that of Christ. The figure at the left of the soldier is a good piece of genre painting; it is a Spanish (or Mexican) peasant in short pants, with a torn white or grey shirt, and barefoot, holding a beaker in his upraised left hand. At the right of the central group is the Centurion, standing rather at ease, holding a tall lance which is almost a vertical line. The most dramatic line is the slightly tipped line of light that extends down the upraised arm of the gambling peasant in the foreground, across the shoulders of his white shirt, and on down to the ground just in front of Christ's feet. All the movement in the two preceding Stations has stopped. This is a dramatic foreshadowing of the Crucifixion itself.

The color is well balanced from left to right against an almost flat, blue-grey sky; the ground is sharp with deep shadows and lights.

Cat. No. 22—Fig. 51.   TENTH STATION

In this painting, the faulty drawing and awkward proportions of the figures is clearly revealed, and the inconsistencies more apparent. There is good drawing in the two peasants.

23. Eleventh Station: Jesus is Nailed to the Cross

This is a fitting contrast to the static character of the preceding Station. The composition is much more open; there is a greater feeling of deep space. The plan is essentially a triangle, with the apex at the prostrate body of the Crucified Christ in the middle of the canvas, the broad base extending across the top. The Cross on which Christ is being nailed lies in a diagonal in the middle distance; space is given by placing a standing Roman soldier in the immediate left foreground, which together with a rock mass, is painted almost in silhouette. This device throws the center of interest into high relief. The now gaunt Christ is outstretched upon the Cross, the hands already nailed to the arms, and the feet being nailed by two men. To the right is another Roman soldier with a spear standing at ease. The vertical line of his figure effectively stops the movement outward, and the face, turned inward, redirects the line to the center. He is in a dull blue tunic with tan-gold cloak and belt. The two men nailing

Cat. No. 23—Fig. 52. ELEVENTH STATION

Christ are stripped bare except for blue cloths about their waists. The body of Christ is nude save for the white loin cloth; this and the pearly luster of the flesh make the dramatic highlights of the composition.

Beyond the head of Christ, and watching from a rock, are three figures painted smaller to give added depth to the composition. On the left is the Blessed Mother in a light blue robe and gown, and next to her is Mary Magdalene in grey, with her head uncovered. The third figure is St. John, in blue with part of a bright red cloak showing. His hands are raised as though in despair.

The landscape setting of rolling hills and rocks is primarily tan and brown up to the single row of distant hills, which are painted in pale blue and grey. The sky is merely a backdrop. There is good forward-backward movement here, and it is a well-organized canvas superior in many respects to others. Its lack of drawing and the stiff posturing prevent the work from achieving a nobility and grandeur that has characterized the paintings of the early schools of both Italy and the Netherlands.

Typical of the repeated anachronisms and inconsistencies of the series is the painting here of the wound in the side of Christ, a bleeding wound from the spear that was not inflicted until after the actual raising of the Cross. The other inconsistencies are in the accompanying figures, the men, the slaves, the soldiers, who rarely appear in the same dress or color throughout the successive scenes. This lack of continuity in depicting the figures accompanying Christ breaks the rhythm of the sequence of the Stations, and makes the mounting tragedy less powerful. The omission of certain figures in successive incidents may have been due to the desire on the part of the artist to avoid overcrowding his compositions.

24. Twelfth Station: Jesus Dies on the Cross

This, the climax of the tragedy, unfortunately is the poorest painting from the standpoint of composition and drawing. In an effort to present the emotion and the suffering of those involved, the artist has presented the three crucified and the three at the foot of the Cross in a close-up. The result is like a section or detail from a larger work.

The composition is based on the intersection of the three vertical lines of the crosses with the horizontal of the center cross and the line of the heads below.

Cat. No. 24—Fig. 53.   TWELFTH STATION

The Crucified Christ, occupying the geometric center, has been represented at the moment just past His death. The figure is relaxed, the head sunk down, the wounds in the chest, knees, and foot still bleeding. The flesh tones here, curiously enough, are more lifelike and natural than they have been in the earlier representations. The crossbar of the Cross is almost at the very top of the canvas; the base of one Cross is below (and outside) the bottom of the canvas.

The penitent thief, on the left, is painted in three-quarter view, the cross here being turned somewhat so that he faces inward toward Christ. The figure, although somewhat out of drawing, is well painted and the flesh tones here are much warmer than that of Christ; the thief has his head raised and his eyes turned heavenward in supplication; he is stripped to the waist; a white shirt is seen above red knee-length pants.

The other crucified figure, the evil thief, is represented in a violent struggle, his body twisted and the arms not nailed but tied behind the post, one foot wrenched free and his knee raised. His face is contorted with hatred, and the whole figure, which is seen almost in profile, is bowed out toward the center. It is almost a direct copy of the thief in the Rubens *Coup de Lance* in Antwerp.

At the bottom are the waist-length figures of the two Marys below the penitent thief and Christ, and St. John between Christ and the wicked thief. Because the figures are all somewhat larger, the artist has here presented emotional expressions. The face of the Blessed Mother, framed in blue, shows only resignation to the Divine Will; there is little sorrow on her face, and her hands are tightly clasped in prayer. To her right, the penitent Magdalen is wiping the tears from her upturned face; the face of St. John, rich and glowing in its color, in great contrast to the others, has a rather dazed, sorrowful look.

The effect of this canvas is in reality a study of facial expressions, but the artist has failed to give to the scene a sense of the tremendous tragedy that has transpired. The too-even illumination of all of the figures has deprived the composition of any rhythmic quality it might have had.

25. Thirteenth Station: The Descent from the Cross

The Deposition is in the tradition of the popular Italian schools of painting. It is a richly colored, well-knit composition, presenting the Blessed Mother half-seated at the foot of the Cross, her right hand outstretched, her face slightly raised heavenward, with the body of Christ in a half-sitting position leaning against her knees. To the right is St. John, and behind him another figure. On the left of

Cat. No. 25—Fig. 54.   THIRTEENTH STATION

Mary is a penitent, her hands clasped in prayer, her face bowed down. The picture is in a very low key. The most dramatic light is in the pattern of an S curve, which begins with the illumined face of Mary and travels down along the head of Christ and along the luminous body, ending almost in the lower right corner, in the head and arms of the Magdalen in the act of wiping the feet of Christ and kissing them.

This is a simple composition, rather rich in color. The deep, full blue of Mary's cloak is an effective background for the pearly luster of the body of Christ. The figure on the left is almost entirely in a brown, or very dull red, and brown-glazed blue. St. John's red cloak or mantle is the only bright color spot.

Considerable attempt has been made to "humanize" the expressions of the persons. The result is an almost overemphasized melodrama, in that the upward slant of the eyebrows of the Sorrowful Mother are a prototype of the much later (nineteenth-century) sentimental romanticism, not only of religious painting but of other work as well. The drawing and painting of the dead Christ in this Station are by far the best of the entire series, and so different that it suggests the hand of another, more skillful painter.

26. Fourteenth Station: The Burial

In this painting there is, appropriately, a return to the almost static lines of the first Station. Again, there is some spatial depth; the tomb is a geometric form set at an angle at a slight distance from the foreground. The two figures in blue, the praying, sorrowful Mother facing front in the left foreground, and a man standing with a lighted torch in his upraised hand in the opposite corner set off the center of the composition. The white, enshrouded body of Christ is being lowered into the tomb by three men. At His feet, and with his back to us, is Joseph of Arimathea in a short red tunic; at the right of the head of Christ is St. John, his bright red cloak setting off the white of the shroud. On the other side of Christ is Nicodemus in a duller, browner red. Thus the artist has framed the Christ first in red, then in blue, and at the periphery, in shadows. The tomb itself is a neutral greenish grey. Mary Magdalen, at the far side of the feet of Christ, is bowed over between Joseph and Mary.

In all, it is a well-balanced, carefully planned composition. The pattern of light and dark, and of color, is thoughtfully handled and most successful.

Cat. No. 26—Fig. 55. FOURTEENTH STATION

27. ST. JOSEPH WITH THE CHRIST CHILD

This painting of St. Joseph, life size, is more Italian in feeling than it is Spanish or Mexican. It is a quiet, dignified and altogether idealized realistic work, simple in its color harmony of grey, green, and browns. It is an excellently painted work, free from the mannerisms of the eighteenth-century school. The influence of Zurburán or Ribera, with the strong modeling and solid painting, is more evident than that of the later Baroque. It is possibly from the studio of Miguel de Herrera.[6]

The painting presents St. Joseph about to walk forward, with the sleeping Christ Child in his right arm, His head against Joseph's shoulder. Joseph holds, with ease, a lily stalk with one white blossom and bud in his left hand. His head is inclined slightly forward.

Dimly seen are various articles of the carpenter shop, a large bucksaw on the left, a sawhorse at the back, and in the lower right corner, a log. The color is very simple. Against a dark, obscure background, Joseph is wearing a dark, almost olive-green, belted tunic, with a cinnamon brown cloak wrapped around him, and carried over his right arm. This brown effectively sets off the grey-blue robe of the child Jesus. The paved floor is grey.

Cat. No. 27—Fig. 56.   ST. JOSEPH AND THE
CHRIST CHILD.   Oil on Canvas.   34x48.

The faces are well and simply painted, as are the hands and feet. The artist has just missed making a sentimental piece. It is a good painting, sound in its craftsmanship, but somehow it lacks a feeling of nobility and mystery. Perhaps this is due to the over-concentration on the subject, especially the nearly sugar-sweetness of the child as He snuggles against Joseph. Joseph is so quiet, almost withdrawn and reserved, and perhaps a greater emotional unity with the child would have lifted this from an ordinary piece into a fine work. It is as though Joseph were conscious of the eternal honor and glory of his role.

The painting is entirely out of key with the others in the Nave. It is in good condition, save for a few surface scratches.

The painting arrived at the Mission on August 12, 1882, being brought there by Father Romo from Mexico.

28. THREE ARCHANGELS

This large, long, horizontal canvas, hung near the St. Francis chapel, is a presentation of three archangels standing on clouds. The figures are full length and in the style of the late Baroque, possibly from the school of José de Ibarra or one of his associates.[7]

On the left stands the winged St. Gabriel, dressed in a splendid, white, fringed tunic, with blue-edged sleeves and blue cords across his chest. A dull greyish-pink cloak flutters behind him, and his head is uncovered. In his left hand he holds a lily stalk with a ribbon on which is inscribed *Ave Maria*. Above the upraised right hand the words *FORTITUDO DEI* are printed in bright vermillion. He is represented in a three-quarter view, facing the center.

The center angel is St. Michael, with left hand raised as though in intercession, the lowered right hand holding a sword. He is dressed in a dove-grey kilt on which are brown bands, and a blue tunic studded

Cat. No. 28—Fig. 57. THREE ARCHANGELS. Oil on canvas. 125x56.

with silver stars. His bright red cape is thrown back and is fluttering, and a dark blue-black cloak falls behind. He wears a silver helmet adorned with feathers, and open-toed boots. Above his left hand is the inscription *QUIS UT DEUS* (Like unto God).

On the right is the figure of St. Raphael, also winged, with the words *MEDICINA DEI* inscribed above his uncovered head. He wears a heavy brownish-tan cloak reaching to the laced boot tops. Over this is an elbow-length grey cape gathered at the neck line. A dull, blue cape over the wings comes across, in front, over his left thigh; two shell-like devices with crossed swords behind, decorate the cape.

The figures represent the saints as young men, and with an idealism characteristic of the early eighteenth century, or Baroque, heroic figures much in the grandiose manner of Callot. They are more theatrical than religious in character. The faces, especially those of Raphael and Gabriel, are curiously feminine in their contours and color. Were it not for the attributes which Gabriel carries with him, the figure would be mistaken for a female angel.

This is a well-painted canvas and the drawing is good. It is essentially a pictorial, two-dimensional composition; the entire background is blue, with a blue-grey cloud or sky. This Mexican painting, is strongly influenced by the "vaporous" style of Murillo, and dates probably from after the mid-eighteenth century. There is no formal organization, merely a representation of three saints with the central figure strongest in color and value.

The painting is mentioned in the Mission inventories of 1835 and 1854.

St. Gabriel. The name signifies "God is my strength," and is the second in rank among the archangels. He is the messenger of God and venerated as the angel who watches over childbirth. Gabriel is highly regarded also by the Jews and the Mohammedans, who regard him as their patron saint. His attributes are the lily, the scroll often inscribed *Ave Maria,* a scepter, and sometimes an olive branch.

St. Michael. The name signifies "like unto God." He is regarded as the first and mightiest of all created spirits. It was he whom God commissioned to expel Satan from Heaven. He is the patron saint of the Church on earth, and lord of the souls of the dead, deciding upon their merits.

St. Michael is the patron saint of France. He is always represented as young and beautiful. As patron of the Church Militant he is the winged saint, with shield and lance. Conqueror of the devil, he is armored, with his foot on the Serpent. As lord of souls, he holds a balance with little naked figures in each scale.

St. Raphael. The name signifies "the medicine of God." He is considered the guardian angel of humanity. He is the protector of the young, the pilgrim and the traveler. He is often presented as a pilgrim, the staff in his hand. As a guardian, he bears the sword and a jar containing the "fishy charm."

29. THE SOULS IN PURGATORY

This painting is a long, horizontal canvas hanging over the St. Francis chapel near the rear of the church. It is a crude, almost primitive work and represents twelve persons, or souls, in Purgatory. The whole canvas is red-vermillion in tone; there is a rough indication of brownish clouds acting somewhat as a frame. The figures are all nude, submerged to the waist in a "sea" or cloud of red. They are freely arranged; some in the attitude of prayer, some with their arms crossed on their chests; two on the left have their right arms raised in supplication. The dominating figure is that of a bishop in the center, his tall silver-grey miter rather conspicuous. On the extreme left is a tonsured friar; near him is a king with a crown on his head. There is a young child and probably a saint with white bandaged head on the brow of which is a red cross.

There is absolutely no pictorial organization save the confluence of the color of flesh, and the darkness of the hair and beards which hold the piece loosely together. Either the painting was never completed or else the work has been damaged to the extent that any color variations have disappeared. It is now on a larger stretcher than it was originally, and evidence of several inches of unpainted canvas can be seen at each end of the work. There is a crack running the length of the piece about one-third of the way up. This, together with the various holes, rips, and punctures attests to the folding of the canvas, probably for transport to the Mission.

It is mentioned in the inventories of 1835 and 1858. There is some possibility that this painting may originally have been at Mission

Cat. No. 29—Fig. 58.   THE SOULS IN PURGATORY.
Oil on canvas. 90x36.

San Carlos (Carmel), for the description by La Pérouse of the works he saw there fits this and its companion piece. There is no record of its date of acquisition to the Santa Barbara Mission.[8]

This type of painting, although literary in content, is typical of the semi-allegorical works used as instructional material by the church. Presumably it presented the fact that all persons, regardless of rank or station or age, could achieve Heaven through the cleansing of Purgatory.

S-30. ST. FRANCIS CHAPEL

The St. Francis Chapel is a small bay in the south wall of the nave near the entrance to the church at the rear. The ceiling is somewhat conical in shape. The walls are decorated with floral-patterned panels separated by painted pilasters and an architectural frieze. The

Cat. No. S-30—Fig. 59.   ST. FRANCIS CHAPEL

dome is painted in narrow "coffers" that converge overhead to imitate a coffered ceiling. The arched entrance is painted on the outside with two supporting pilasters connected by a continuous "marbleized" arch with a cross at the place of the keystone. There is a heavy leaf pattern border outside the arch design proper.

The altar in the chapel is extremely simple, similar to the main altar and the two side ones near the sanctuary. It is made of cement. A full-length figure of St. Francis, his arms folded across the breast, stands on top of the altar. It is 47½ inches tall, and a very good example of modern devotional sculpture in polychromed wood.

The decoration of this chapel, though in harmony with the remainder of the interior of the church, is much more sophisticated and is in no sense a restoration of Indian work. Most of the design has been applied by stencil. The chapel is about twelve feet wide and eight and one half feet deep.

31. THE SOULS IN HELL

A companion piece to the Souls in Purgatory, this painting hangs over the St. Anthony chapel directly opposite. It also has a predominantly red-orange color, with darkish clouds and vapors. This, because of the greater number of figures, results in more of an all-over pattern. There is no principal center of interest. Some of the damned souls are painted larger than others; the devils are sometimes shown in full length, as satyr-like creatures, principally in browns. The different punishments for the various sins are depicted. All the souls are in extreme distress, agitated and disturbed, but the artist failed to make the punishment convincing in spite of the Hounds of Hell, the prison bars, the serpents eating out breasts, the dragons and the smoke, fire, and horrible grimaces.

Cat. No. 31—Fig. 60. THE SOULS IN HELL. Oil on canvas. 90x36.

It is a seventeenth-century version of the old medieval pieces. Here the craftsmanship of the artist has failed, and the effect of the whole, although rather startling, is amusing rather than terrifying. However, the impression of such a work on the Indians may have been considerable.

The painting has a long, horizontal crack. It appears to be on the original stretcher.

It is mentioned in the inventories of 1835 and 1858. It is possible that this, together with the Purgatory, was originally at Carmel Mission, as was mentioned earlier. (See also Note 8.)

32. THREE WOMEN SAINTS

This painting, a long horizontal, is the companion piece to that of the Archangels, across from which it hangs in the Nave.

As in its counterpart, the three figures are on clouds; there is only empty space behind them. Here, however, the heads of infant angels appear through the clouds in the upper corners and above at each side of the center figure. There is no compositional relationship between the three women. All are facing in the same three-quarter direction, making for even less unity than in the painting of the Archangels. However, this painting is sounder, and the whole is a superior work.

The figure on the left is probably St. Agnes of Assisi. Her habit has a black cowl and a white wimple. She carries, or holds without a feeling of weight, the Infant Jesus in her right arm. The Infant, sitting upright, is clothed in a rose-colored garment; both hands are outstretched; His hair is light golden brown. The saint looks adoringly at Him. There is very good painting here, solid and firm, with character and a fine understanding of modeling. So also is the head of Jesus, a rather charming and beautiful child without being sentimental. The device of the Saint holding the Christ Child is a derivation from Murillo, who painted St. Rose of Lima holding the Infant Savior.[9]

St. Clare, (founder of the Poor Clares), the center figure, stands full length looking upward and outward and slightly toward the left. She is clothed exactly as is the saint to the left. She holds in her right hand an ostensorium or pyx, containing the Host, around the base of which is a linen cloth, and her left hand, likewise holding the cloth, supports the base of the ostensorium. A tall, curved, and gilded Abbess' crozier leans in the crook of her left arm, the curve of the crozier complementing the oval of her face. The robes are very full and voluminous. The color is a dull, dark, brown.

St. Margaret of Cortona, on the right, kneels facing toward the center and gazing intently upon a crucifix, the upper portion of which she holds in her right hand close to her face. The long staff of the crucifix rests in the palm of her left hand. Unlike the other two saints, her head is swathed in white, and the white cowl comes down almost covering her shoulders. At her feet, to the right, are a skull and what appear to be thongs for flagellation, both the symbols of penance.

This figure is perhaps the best and most directly painted of those in the nave of the church. The figure is treated as a flatly modeled, pyramidal mass, the light and dark areas being simply handled and giving to the whole a monumental character that is lacking in many of the other works. The whole shadow mass, from the top of the head to the feet behind her, is a continuous band of dark, a dark which is repeated on the opposite side of the figure where the shadow of the extended arm falls down the length of the body. This makes for a strikingly effective work, almost modern in feeling.

The clouds and the little angels emerging from them are obviously derived from the Murillo school. The cloud colors vary; behind the heads of the three saints it is golden tan; lower down and at the sides, they are blue-grey. A rather plastic sense of space is achieved by making the foreground clouds almost white. There is little modeling. Continued study of the painting increases the feeling of space and floating.

Cat. No. 32—Fig. 61. THREE WOMEN SAINTS. Oil on canvas. 162x55.

This is a good work, and dates probably from the middle of the eighteenth century. The painting is mentioned in the inventories of 1835, 1854, and 1858.

St. Agnes of Assisi was the younger sister of St. Clare, and was born about 1198. She adopted a life of poverty, and was later chosen by St. Francis to found and govern a community of Poor Clares near Florence. She established several monasteries in the north of Italy. Her death took place in 1252 or 1253.

St. Clare of Assisi, founder of the Poor Clares and first Abbess of San Damiano, was born on July 16, 1194, at Assisi. She took the vows with St. Francis. After some time with the Benedictine Nuns, she and St. Agnes removed to a small house where her congregation gradually increased. She governed this small community for forty years, being ill for some twenty-seven years of the time. She obtained the privilege of extreme poverty, of living solely on alms. The Order has since been known as the Poor Clares, a rigorous and self-disciplining order. Her Order spread far beyond Italy by the time of her death in 1253. She was canonized in 1255. St. Clare is a favorite saint in Europe, and especially in Spain. Her proper attribute is the pyx containing the Host. She wears a grey tunic, a black veil, and the cord of St. Francis. She also bears the lily, the cross, and the palm.

St. Margaret of Cortona was born in Tuscany in 1249. She was a penitent of the Third Order, under the guidance of the Franciscan Friars of Cortona. She was converted in 1274, and two years later was admitted to the Third Order of St. Francis. She founded a hospital for the poor and a congregation of Tertiary Sisters (Poverelle). She died on February 22, 1297, and was canonized in 1328. Her feast day is February 22. She is usually painted as young and beautiful, her dress not always that of the nun, but usually with the cord for a girdle. Her attribute is a dog.

33. OUR LADY OF GUADALUPE

This is a large, almost life-sized, well-executed copy of the famous Mexican Guadalupe, in oil on canvas. The Virgin stands on a dark crescent moon, below which is the head of an angel. The painting has many horizontal cracks, probably the result of its having been removed from its stretcher and incorrectly rolled. It was brought to the Mission from Mexico by Father Romo between 1872 and 1885. It is signed "J. C. Padilla F." in the lower right corner. Padilla was

Cat. No. 33.—*Fig. 62.* OUR LADY OF GUADALUPE.
Oil on canvas. 47x69.

a minor Mexican painter active probably during the early years of the nineteenth century.

Although considerably the worse for wear, much of the coloring of the original glazes remains. It is very carefully executed, and the pigment is applied thinly and evenly. The warm, rather dusky flesh tones of the Virgin's face and hands contrast effectively with the soft, muted pink of her robe and the deep blue of her cloak. Gold stars stud this cloak, while an elaborate floral design suggesting a heavy damask, also in gold, covers the robe. This pattern lies almost flat across the area, scarcely following the modeling of the body underneath.

The figure is surrounded by golden rays which are painted against a darker ground. The entire figure and its rays are enclosed by an irregularly scalloped area in reddish brown. Beneath the crescent supporting the Virgin is the figure of a young angel, who, clothed in a dull pink, holds up the crescent moon. His wings are beautifully colored in bands of dark blue, buff, and orange.

This work is a copy of the famous picture at Guadalupe-Hidalgo, some three miles northeast of Mexico City. The painting is taken as representing the Immaculate Conception, being the lone figure of "the Woman with sun, moon, and star accompaniments of the great apocalyptic sign," and a supporting angel under the crescent. Its tradition is long-standing. On December 9, 1531, the Blessed Virgin appeared to one Juan Diego, an Indian neophyte, on a hill side some distance from the city. She sent him to Bishop Zumarraga to have a temple built where she stood. She was at the same place that evening and the next to receive the answer of the Bishop, who did not believe the messenger Juan, and who finally bade him ask for a sign of the lady who said she was the Mother of God. Juan agreed to this, but because of the critical illness of an uncle, attempted to bypass the meeting place, but the Blessed Virgin crossed down to meet him. She reassured Juan, and bade him go again to the Bishop, whereupon he asked her for a sign. He was told to gather roses, which she arranged in his cloak, bidding him to keep them untouched and unseen until he reached the Bishop. As he unfolded his cloak, the roses fell from it and the life-sized figure of the Virgin as she appeared to Juan was glowing on the cloak.

The coarsely woven stuff which bears the original picture is like burlap, and was probably made of maguey fiber. It consists of two strips about 18 by 70 inches long, stitched together. The seam is visible up to the middle of the figure, turning aside from the face. Painters have not understood the laying on of the colors nor the unprepared canvas, but marvel at the apparent oil and distemper coloring. There are flowerlike tints and abundant gold. The chief colors are deep gold in the rays and the stars, deep blue-green in the mantle, and rose in the flowered robe.

A canonical inquiry was instituted in 1556 to determine the authenticity of the painting. The picture, as well as the shrine which has been built around it, is the center of numerous pilgrimages. Our Lady of Guadalupe became the national patron of Mexico, and December 12 became a holy day of obligation in Mexico.

34. THE CRUCIFIXION

This, with the Coronation of the Virgin opposite to which it hangs, is the largest canvas in the church, and one of the few large pieces in the Mission.

Cat. No. 34—Fig. 63. THE CRUCIFIXION.
Oil on canvas. 126x168.

It is a simply planned work in two principal planes; the Crucified Christ on the center, the Sorrowful Mother standing on the left, the Magdalen embracing the foot of the Cross, and St. John standing right. The ground is a rocky terrain; in the background is a silhouette of towers of a city, about one-half way up the canvas. Above the city and behind the heads of Mary and St. John is a stormy blue-black sky.

The Christ is very well painted; there is the supernatural and beyond-earthly color of the flesh that illumines the whole canvas. The figure does not sag heavily from the arms of the Cross, but rather suggests imminent flight upward, and at the same time a sweeping benediction that goes over and beyond the three figures below him. Yet there is no "support" from color or light. The bleeding wounds, and the blood-stained loincloth are in keeping with the more melo-dramatic aspects of Spanish art. The posturing of the Blessed Mother at the left, with her left hand at the breast and her right hand thrust outward, and the almost similar pose of St. John opposite is characteristic of the "operatic" poses of almost all larger religious works dating from after the middle of the seventeenth century, and especially of Spanish work, resulting in a theatrical rather than a dramatic work.

Though this is Spanish-style art, it is more similar to the Flemish type of Crucifixion, in composition at least. The very personal physical suffering of the individuals remains typical of Spanish art. More care is given to facial expressions of sorrow than is given to the entire composition. Here unity is achieved, as it so frequently was in Gothic times, through the use of directing gestures and (as even in the case of some Leonardos) through pointing. Hence, the spectator is forced to become absorbed and influenced by the reactions of the persons at the scene, here the two Marys and St. John, rather than at the Crucifixion.[10]

This painting was listed in the inventories of 1835 and 1858.

S-35. THE *PIETA*

Though this is a very recent addition to the Mission, it is without question the oldest, and in many respects the most simply beautiful of all the sculptured pieces. The figure, of carved white alabaster, with painted details and a four-inch crown atop her head, is about twenty-one inches high on a five and one half inch base. There is no indication of a seat, and the Sorrowful Mother stands behind the body of Christ, lying across a short bier.

The sculpture has, roughly, two parts: one, the creamy yellow, almost rectangular lower portion comprising the body of Christ and the gown of Mary, and the upper portion, which is an almost equilateral triangle of the body, arms, shoulders, and head, with the enveloping mantle insisting the triangle. The upper portion of the figure is rather stiff, presenting Mary as a richly gowned woman, the pattern gown fitting very tightly, producing a wasp-like pinched-in waist, and a bulge out to the hips.

The simple features of the Virgin are carved out of the same material, almost free of detail. The eyes, which are mere slits set at angles under slightly overhanging brows, are remarkable for their expressiveness. They are very nearly almond-shaped slits; the pupils, which are dark and deeply cut, look as though there may have been insets at one time. The very small mouth is partly open; the nose is

Cat. No. S-35—Fig. 64. THE *PIETA*. Polychromed alabaster. 30″.

exquisitely carved. The face is one of the loveliest and simplest of its type and reveals somehow an inner sorrow.

The figure of the mutilated Christ is quite angular, clearly describing the geometric block from which it was carved. The head is to the left; the knees at the right of the block, and the lower legs fall perpendicularly down. There is some distortion in the figure —distortion in the leanness and accentuated angularity. The head of Christ is slightly turned, chin upward; the chest is an almost horizontal line, while the abdomen sags abruptly inward to the horizontal line of the thigh. The right arm lies easily along the side, and the hand curves downward into the folds of the robe on which He lies.

Cat. No. S-35
Fig. 65.   THE SORROWFUL MOTHER.
Detail of Fig. 64.

From the top of Mary's head a heavy mantle falls, completely enclosing her, falling over each arm as far as the wrists, and then dropping down on each side almost to the floor. The alabaster here, as in other parts, has been covered with a layer of gesso and painted black. A pattern of simple, geometric flowers and a border of grapes and acanthus or vine leaves have been applied in gilt.

Mary's gown, which covers her throat, and which has very long, gathered-at-the-wrist sleeves, has a chevron pattern carved into it, and there is no indication of wrinkles or folds in any part of the garment. It had been painted, probably a dull gold (i.e., gold-leafed). There is a V-shaped band ending at the waist showing traces of having been painted dark. The torso is almost fully round, the space between the arms and the body closed at the back by the cloak. The hands, one of which extends over the head of Christ and the other over His knees, are partly broken off at the fingers. Unlike the face and body, they are exquisitely carved in detail, even to the finger nails. Originally they were of one piece; evidence of patching or repairing is in the bits of wire inserted to hold fingers. The fingers originally projected slightly beyond and over the body of Christ. It appears that the "cloth," or linen, on which Christ's body rests was at one time also covered with gesso; flakes of this substance, now a dirty brown, are still in evidence in the folds and crevices.

The crown resting on the head of the Sorrowing Mother is probably of marble or alabaster and is covered with a coat of gesso and gold leaf. "Jewels" in relief were formerly colored.

What makes this little statue remarkable is the sharp contrasts between the simple, decorative formalism of the torso and arms of the body of the Virgin, with its rather stiff pose, standing with outstretched arms, and the realistically carved Christ. It appears almost as if the two figures had been separately carved, so unlike are they in treatment, there being so much more detail in Christ than in His Mother.

The figure group rests on a carved pedestal of what seems to be brownish marble, about five inches high, and some thirteen to fourteen inches long. There are insets of colored chalcedony, or brown agate, set into small panels along the base of the pedestal; most of these have dropped out, leaving rectangular depressions. The center of the pedestal is dominated by a carved "medallion" of quite similar agate-like material, in the form of leaf and scroll shapes, very simply cut. It too is cemented to the face of the pedestal.

This small work is undoubtedly of Spanish origin and probably dates from the fifteenth century. The influence of the Flemish school is clearly felt in the angularity; it has some resemblance, in feeling rather than in appearance, to the famous Avignon *Pietà*.

This piece was a gift to the Mission in 1928 or 1929.

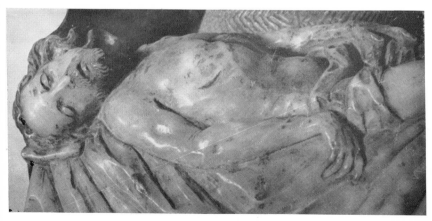

Cat. No. S-35—Fig. 66.   THE DEAD CHRIST. Detail of Fig. 64.

36. THE BAPTISM OF CHRIST

This oil on canvas is one of the better paintings in the Mission collection. It differs from nearly every other painting in that the figures, though dominating, are set within a carefully painted landscape. Though the bluish green coloring prevails, and there are present the delicate flesh tones and the reds so characteristic of late seventeenth-century Mexican painting, the general quality and composition recall the Italian paintings of Verrocchio, and were it not for the presence of the angels and God the Father in the sky, it might be mistaken for a copy or adaptation of such.

The scene represents John the Baptist kneeling on a rock, leaning over toward Christ, who stands somewhat below him in a stream. St. John is pouring the water from a shell with his raised

Cat. No. 36—Fig. 67. THE BAPTISM OF CHRIST.
Oil on canvas. 35x45.

right hand. He is clothed in a scant, tattered grey garment. Over his right shoulder and gathered over the thighs is a bright red mantle. His left hand, extended downwards, holds a thin staff with a cross entwined with a narrow grey ribbon at the top.

Christ stands almost directly in the center of the symmetrical composition, His arms folded across the chest, the body slightly turned, the weight on the left leg. The beautifully painted, bearded face, framed in flowing hair, is turned slightly to one side and downward. The figure is nude save for a loosely draped white garment at the waist. Both figures are very well executed but have the appearance of having been copied from some superior model and superimposed on a background.

The setting is a winding stream in a hilly landscape, with the walls of a medieval city and mountains and trees in the distance, a characteristic notable in Italian painting as early as the Baptism by Masolino (1383-1447). Directly across the top of-the composition is the figure of God the Father emerging, somewhat abruptly, from the clouds, with His hands raised in benediction, and looking down on the scene directly below Him. The dove hovers between Him and the head of Christ. To each side are the heads of young angels.

The painting has a silvery grey-blue tonality, with strong blue-greens in the water, trees, and hills. The red robe of God the Father is a faint echo of the rich red on St. John. The painting is a curious composition in a plastic sense. There is no feeling of planes or solidity in the landscape; depth is achieved more or less through value changes and slight color gradations. The two principal figures are in the immediate foreground, and though the rest is painted in perspective, it serves to act rather as a two-dimensional back drop in spite of its apparent realism. The brushwork and modeling of the figures is not the same as that of the other portions of the canvas.

The painting of the heads and the expression on their faces are very similar to those in the large Coronation of the Virgin (Figure 40). The general style and coloring and the firmness of the drawing suggest that it might be from the studio of Ibarra or Cabrera.

This work was sent from Mexico on February 19, 1802, and was at the Mission by December 31 of that year. It is mentioned only in the inventory of 1858.

37. OUR LORD, ACCORDING TO ST. LUKE

This large canvas, a full-length figure of Christ with God the Father and the Holy Spirit above Him and with small angels in the clouds is signed and dated in the lower right-hand corner: "Joseph de Páez, fecit Mexico a. 1765." Along the bottom of the canvas, in an irregular medallion, is the following lettered inscription, the title of the painting: "Forma y traxe de CHRISTO SENOR NUESTRO, conforme escrivió San Anselmo y retrató San Lucas."

This is a fine work. Christ, painted as a man in his late twenties, stands firmly in a rocky, arboreal landscape. The form is monumental, assuming an almost pyramidal form. The robe of Christ is a rich, dark brown; it appears to be an ankle-length tunic over which is worn a long cloak with very full sleeves of the same color and texture. The head is well painted in a direct, straightforward manner. The eyes look out and somewhat downward. The rich, very dark brown hair falls to the shoulders; there is a short beard. A quiet expression shows Christ in the prime of His manhood; there is no trace of sentimentalism. The one hand revealed is holding a fold of the cloak.

The Godhead above looking down upon Him, hands raised in blessing, is beautifully painted. Here the hair and beard are grey. God appears from out of a cloud, and from Him issues the Dove. His left elbow rests on a blue globe, and in His left hand He holds a small thick stick. He is clothed in a grey-white robe with a rose-colored scarf around His right arm and fluttering behind Him.

At the left edge of the clouds are three baby angels in the style of Murillo, looking on in adoration, and on the opposite side are three more. They are not too successfully presented.

The Lord stands against a dull blue-grey sky which shades off to a rosy cast on the horizon. The rocky scene, with its waterfall and its trees, is reminiscent of Umbrian landscapes; the trees look like those from a Titian background.

There seems, however, to be slight relationship between the great figure and its setting; the artist has painted the Lord against the scene rather than within it. As is so often the case in paintings of this type, the lighting is confused; light appears to be coming from above and to the left from outside the canvas, similarly illuminating the faces and the hands of God the Father and the Lord, as well as the six angels, but this light never reaches the landscape, and there is, hence, no form or modeling. The result is that Christ seems to be floating in, or painted against, the scene.

Formu y traxe de CHRISTO SEÑOR NUESTRO conforme escrivió San
Anselmo y retrató San Lucas.

Cat. No. 37—Fig. 68. OUR LORD ACCORDING TO ST. LUKE.
Oil on canvas. 61x94.

The coloring, and the introduction of the Father and the Dove to make clear the divine character of Christ are other devices made use of by many Spanish painters. It is this overstatement of fact that prevents paintings of this type from attaining greatness, for they tend, as did so many of the Murillos, to become trivial in spite of their themes and subjects.

The canvas is in fair condition, although bruised and scarred. There is a sharp crack entirely across the canvas just above the middle and another about one-quarter of the way up. Two very large tears and rips are in the lower right-hand quarter; several abrasions and holes are scattered throughout.

The painting was received, according to a letter from Fr. Romo, some time in 1882. Up to 1925, it hung on the left wall of the Sanctuary. It is now in the Sacristy.

Cat. No. 37—Fig. 69. HEAD OF OUR LORD.
Detail of Fig. 68.

38. MISSION SAN CARLOS BORROMEO

This painting of the Carmel Mission is very well executed in the rather conventional, somewhat romantic style of the late nineteenth century, solidly painted in what might be termed the post-Hudson River School of American landscape. It is far superior to the majority of other late nineteenth-century paintings of the various missions to be seen throughout California. The canvas is signed "M. Dahlgren."

The ruined Mission is seen from the rear (the southwest), and clearly shows the unusual arch construction of the nave of the church, the partially collapsed tile roof, and the almost total ruin of the back portion of the church. In the distance can be seen the remains of the walls that once were part of the Mission compound. Beyond are the tree covered hills and a stormy, rain-swept sky. Three figures, one of which appears to be a priest, stand in the middle distance. The foreground is a mass of blooming flowers and wild grasses.

The canvas is in good condition save for dulled varnishes. It is in an extremely heavy and ornate frame that in itself is a museum piece.

Cat. No. 38—Fig. 70. MISSION SAN CARLOS BORROMEO.
Oil on canvas. 35x20.

PAINTINGS ON COPPER

This group of paintings, each of which is 11½ inches high, and 16⅜ inches wide, is arranged in the form of a cross and enclosed within one large frame. These paintings are on copper and are unfortunately in very poor condition, for the pigments have flaked off in considerable areas, and elsewhere have faded exceedingly. Throughout, the predominant colors are blues and greens. Much of the luminous quality of this group of paintings has been dulled by the brown and yellow varnishes that have darkened with age. They are probably early eighteenth century.

This group of paintings was a present to the Mission in 1924.

Fig. 71. PAINTINGS ON COPPER

39. CHRIST AT THE WELL OF JACOB
Figure 71, top.

This is a Rubens-like composition, rather exuberant in its movement. The well in the center has a heavy wood lowering bucket. This rectangle serves to stabilize and unify the composition and contrasts the curved lines of the two women on the right and Christ and his followers on the left.

The setting is in a rocky place outside a town, the Gothic-like towers and battlements of which can be seen in the distance. Christ is seated at the left of the wall; the women stand at the right. Behind Christ is a closely knit group of men.

The colors of this work are very badly faded and heavily dis-colored from varnishes; it had at one time a blue-green cast with soft tans and ochres and patches of clear blue and red.

Although not the work of a first-rate painter, this painting shows a thorough knowledge of composition. The composition is static, well balanced, yet perhaps too spotty. It is probably a "school" work, perhaps from that of José de Ibarra, and shows a strong eighteenth-century French influence. The face of the woman and her fluttering gown recall the extravagant court ballet of Paris and other capitals of that period.

40. CHRIST AT THE HOME OF SIMON

Figure 71, center.

This composition occupies the center portion of the cruciform frame. At first glance this suggests the famous Last Supper by Tin-toretto. It has some of the baroque movement but is much more restrained. The elaborate stage effect is evident in the gathered draperies, the arches and pillars, and the short vistas through the open doors. The central figure, Christ, in blue robes, is seated well to the left at a long oval table, and directly before Him is the Magdalen washing His feet. His right hand is raised in blessing. Around the table are eight figures, some watching the Christ, others conversing or eating. Here a good circular movement in composition exists; the ellipse is contrasted by the standing figures of three servants.

The colors are in very poor condition; again clear blue dominates; touches of flesh pink, rose, and beige create a pattern. There are some obviously early eighteenth-century French touches in the bloom of the cheeks and the hands and even in the feet of the Savior, which recall more the boudoir painting of a Nattier than a religious painting.

41. CHRIST'S ENTRY INTO JERUSALEM

Figures 71, bottom, and 72.

In contrast to Numbers 39 and 40 of this group, this painting is more panoramic in concept, and although obviously of the same period and studio, its composition hearks back to the multi-scened Gothic paintings of Italy and France.

Cat. No. 41—Fig. 72. CHRIST'S ENTRY INTO JERUSALEM. From Fig. 71.

The scene presents Christ in blue, on a brown donkey, surrounded by a palm-bearing crowd. The picture is crowded; the group of figures surrounding Christ are massed in the foreground. In the upper left some of the people are stripping palm branches from trees. The upper portion of the painting is a view of hilly country, a long expanse of water with mountains beyond, and a town to the left. At the right, considerably below the group, is the walled city, whose buildings are a combination of classical and medieval architecture.

The painting is in very poor condition. Most of the colors are badly faded and yellowed, and have flaked off from the copper base. What remains are dull blues, yellow-greens and soft reds.

42. CHRIST ASLEEP IN THE BOAT

Figure 71, right.

Christ reclines asleep in the bow of a storm-tossed sailboat which is crowded with nine fishermen, one of whom is attempting to furl the sail. In the distance are other boats under a storm-clouded sky, and on the shore to the right, an elaborate "classical" city.

The composition is full of movement, the pattern of light on the arms of the figures, and the wave caps, although rather crudely executed, show the influence of Tintoretto. As in most of these paintings, the technical aspects of the work are inconsistent, there being surprisingly good work in some of the heads in contrast to the nearly careless painting of the waves and other details.

It is very soiled and dull, the predominant colors being the blues and blue-greens of the water and the sky, and the flesh tones of the faces and bare arms.

43. CHRIST WALKING ON THE WATERS

Figures 71, left, and 73.

This painting also has a semi-primitive Gothic-like composition. In the center is the large figure of Christ leading Peter to the safety of the shore on the left. Behind them is the crowded boat, and beyond it another boat about to leave the shore. The work is similar to others in the group, but here, however, the water has a very solid appearance. There is some understanding of perspective, although the scale of figures is very inconsistent.

Cat. No. 43—Fig. 73. CHRIST ON THE WATERS. From Fig. 71

The walking Christ is in a brown tunic with a blue cloak; Peter, who is kneeling at the right of Christ, wears a blue robe with a brown cloak. The dominant color of the picture is the blue and blue-green on both water and sky. There are large patches of yellowed varnish that nearly obscure the painting. The brush work of the water is a bit better than that in the storm-tossed boat.

44. THE VIRGIN OF THE APOCALYPSE

The painting represents the figure of the Virgin standing with her right foot on the head or heads of a dragon that has been chained or collared.

The Virgin stands in a characteristically Baroque pose, in a three-quarter position, looking at the dragon over her right shoulder. In her hands she holds the Infant Child, who is turning up and away, one arm around her neck, the other raised. The Virgin has grey wings; above her is God the Father emerging from clouds, and beneath Him, the Dove. His head is surrounded by a triangular nimbus. God holds a small, carved wand in His left hand; His right is raised in blessing the scene below. On the left of the canvas the Archangel Michael in seventeenth-century tunic and robes, standing on a rock, grasps the end of a chain fastened to the subdued dragon. His hair is light brown with a band having a small cross.

Cat. No. 44—

Fig. 74. THE VIRGIN OF THE APOCALYPSE. Oil on canvas. 30x37.

At the right, seated among rocks in the distance, is the bearded St. John of Patmos, holding a book in his right hand and a quill pen in the left. His head is raised to look toward Mary. On the ground beside him is the eagle, its head turned toward him, and carrying what might be the inkstand in its beak.

The composition proper is enclosed in an oval area with the four corners of the canvas painted out in brown. It appears to have been originally somewhat larger, for the oval is not complete, and the canvas is remounted. It is probably an early eighteenth-century work.

The painting is well conceived but irregular in its draftsmanship and execution. The heads of God the Father and that of St. John are inferior in drawing and execution to the work on the Virgin. The principal colors are blues, blue-greens, silvery greys, and warm reds, with delicate flesh tones.

The canvas is badly damaged, with many abrasions and small tears, and has been remounted. There is no record of its acquisition to the mission.[11]

Paintings of the Virgin of the Apocalypse, often called the Winged Madonna, are comparatively rare. They appear most frequently in Spanish and Mexican art. The theme of the painting is taken from the Twelfth Chapter of the Apocalypse, verse 1, which reads in part: ". . . a woman clothed with the sun, and the moon was under her feet, and upon her head a crown of twelve stars." The presence of the wings is explained in verse xiv: "And there were given to the woman the two wings of the great eagle, that she might fly into the wilderness unto her place. . . ."

45. FATHER JOSE GONZALES RUBIO

Cat. No. 45—
Fig. 75. FATHER JOSE GONZALES RUBIO. Oil on canvas. 31x39.

This oil on canvas is one of the very few portraits in the Mission collection. It is a large canvas showing Father Rubio as a vigorous man in the prime of life seated at a desk, pausing from his writing in a large book. He is wearing the Franciscan habit and the tonsure.

The portrait is a very good piece of work in the general tradition of commissioned works. It was painted in 1850 by the Italian artist L. Barbieri and was restored in 1906 by Robert Wagner after it had been damaged. It was the gift of the people of Santa Barbara to the Padre. The tribute lettered in the lower right corner is translated as follows:

The Most Illustrious Father José María de Jesús Gonzales Rubio of the Franciscan Order, Ruler of the Diocese of Both Californias, which the people of Santa Barbara had painted in testimony of their warm affection and public appreciation and which is to be preserved as a precious memorial of his eminent virtues and as a grateful memento of his unquenchable charity towards the poor and his love for everyone.

Father Rubio was born June 6, 1804, at Guadalajara. He became a Franciscan in 1824 and in 1830 joined the Missionary College of Guadalupe near Zacatecas for the purpose of serving in the California Missions. He arrived at Monterey in 1833 and was assigned to Mission San José until 1842 when he went to Santa Barbara to serve as secretary to Bishop Diego García. After the death of the Bishop, he became administrator of the Diocese. García's successor, Alemany, appointed him vicar general in 1850. Meanwhile he also served as parish priest for the community. He became superior of the Santa Barbara Missionary College until the arrival of Father Romo in 1872. He died, the last survivor of the California missionaries, as a man loved and respected by all from the beginning to the end of his career, on November 2, 1875. He is buried in the vaults of the Mission cemetery.

46. ST. JOSEPH AND THE CHRIST CHILD

This oil on canvas, recently discovered at the Mission, is undoubtedly an early eighteenth-century work from a Mexican school or studio. It is similar in style and in its proportions of the figures to the Fourteen Stations of the Cross.

The painting presents Joseph, seated, with the Christ Child resting against his left arm. The drawing is somewhat out of proportion, the head of Joseph being quite large in relation to the body; otherwise the drawing and the painting is fairly accurate. It is simply painted. The colors are now dulled by age, but there are spots of remaining brilliance. Joseph is clothed in a collared, short-sleeved, blue-grey tunic tied with a carefully drawn bow knot at the waist. The long sleeves of an under tunic are brilliant red-orange. Over this is a loosely thrown brown cloak. The Christ Child is in a soft pink robe. The hair of the child is painted golden; that of Joseph is long and soft brown, and his face is bearded.

The poses are very nearly romantic-sentimental, and though the composition is good, and it is a fair piece of work, the expressions of the two faces are rather inane. The head of Joseph is turned slightly to the left; the heavy lidded brown eyes look off into space. The Christ Child holds a cross in His right hand, the left outstretched, and the head turned upward with the eyes also looking upward. The flesh tones are pink and rather artificial in character.

Joseph holds his traditional long staff, the top of which has burst into a group of three five-petaled white flowers, in the extreme upper left-hand corner of the painting.

The background is the conventional vague space, except for a mass of clouds on which the figures are seated, a device, which along with the pinkish tones of the flesh, dates the work as a mid-eighteenth-century reinterpretation of Mexican Baroque. There are evidences of red-orange or vermillion underpainting in several areas, especially in the garment of the Christ Child. It is painted on a fairly coarse linen canvas.

In the extreme lower right-hand corner there is a signature: "Ayala Fv." Ignacio Ayala was one of a group of minor painters active in and around Mexico City during the middle and the end of the eighteenth century. His style resembles somewhat the work of Juan Correa.

Cat. No. 46—
Fig. 76. ST. JOSEPH AND THE CHRiST
CHILD. Oil on canvas. 17x22.

Cat. No. 47—
Fig. 77.   BISHOP GARCIA Y DIEGO.
Tinted photograph. 14x19.

47. BISHOP GARCIA Y DIEGO

The portrait of the first Bishop of the Californias is a tinted photograph made probably from the original in Mexico (Zacatecas).[12] The subject is shown in a three-quarter pose. It is an excellently painted likeness of the man whose sorrowful eyes look out from a very well modeled head. He is shown wearing a white cassock and white skull cap, and a heavy silver or ivory cross.

The painting from which this was made is oval in form, and the lettering surrounding the oval has the following inscription: "EL ILLMO. Y RMO. S.D.F. FRANCISCO GARCIA DIEGO, PRIMER OBPO. DE CALIFORNIAS."

48. SANTA BARBARA MISSION

This small watercolor by J. S. Alden, painted in 1855, is one of the earliest paintings of the Mission. It is a rather stiff work, executed in soft colors. To the right is a group of adobe and tile-roofed buildings and a low wall enclosing a garden, behind which appear tents or other small buildings. The long enclosure wall on the left has its counterpart today.

The entire foreground of the Mission "plaza" is devoid of any trees. There is a group of figures in the center foreground. The

Cat. No. 48—Fig. 78. MISSION SANTA BARBARA. Watercolor. 17x8.

sculptures on the typanum, of Faith, Hope, and Charity, are missing. This watercolor also shows a door on the ground floor of each of the two towers, a product, no doubt, of his imagination. The steps leading to the corridor are missing. There is also what appears to be an open corridor above the arched one, immediately under the tiled roof.

49. MISSION SANTA BARBARA

This small oil painting was executed by Ferdinand Dieppa in May, 1832, and is the earliest known representation of this Mission. It is typical of the works of minor artists and amateurs who painted the "romantic missions." The most that can be said for works of this type is that they serve as an indication of the appearance of the missions at the time they were painted. Too often, however, the painters took liberties or misinterpreted what was before them. This is a remarkably accurate representation.

Cat. No. 49—Fig. 79. MISSION SANTA BARBARA. Oil on canvas. 13x9.

S-50. ST. ANTHONY AND THE INFANT JESUS

St. Anthony carrying the Infant Jesus is a polychromed wood carving about twenty-four inches high. It is similar in character and execution to the St. Francis and St. Dominic of the Reredos in the Sanctuary. This is a remarkably fine and expressive piece, probably end of the seventeenth-century Mexican.

He carries the Infant in the crook of his right arm and gives him added support with the left hand. There is a white "cloth" on which the child sits which falls in easy folds to the Saint's waist and gives a good contrast of color. The Infant has an orange-brown, sleeved tunic and a dark blue robe. He holds the scripture in His left hand; the right is upraised.

The saint has a lean, angular face with the planes strongly accented and a rather curious expression because of the manner in

Cat. No. S-50—Fig. 80.   ST. ANTHONY AND THE
INFANT JESUS. Polychromed wood. 23″.

which the eyes are set, the upper lids being extremely large and
heavy and very nearly continuous with the brow. The eyes themselves
are painted a rich, dark brown, giving to the face a limpid, full look.
The hair, as is that of the Infant, is a simply massed, close-cropped
head of curls, although few details are presented. The expression on
on the Infant's face is conventional, rather blank, and is that of a
small man rather than of a child. The color finish of the whole is
highly lustrous and in very good condition.

It is the posture of the saint that gives to the figure its charm
and character. He stands, resting easily on the right foot, with the
left somewhat forward; the folds of his habit fall in simple perpendicular
lines from the waist on each side of the projecting knee.

The left arm of the statue has been repaired, for it had been
broken off at the wrist. The enamel-like coloring of the faces and
hands is remarkably fresh in color; it may very well have been restored.

This sculpture is likely the piece longest in the Mission, for Engelhardt mentions that "Among the church goods acquired this year [1790] was a statue of St. Anthony. It was about three feet in height and stood on a pedestal."[13] The date of acquisition was April 1, 1790. It is mentioned in the invoice of 1856.

St. Anthony of Padua was a Portuguese by birth and became a Franciscan missionary in Morocco to convert the Moors. Illness forced his return to Italy, where he came to Assisi. He became a great teacher and preacher and very popular in France and in Italy. He died at the age of thirty-six, on June 13, 1231.

He is usually pictured with the Infant Jesus standing on his book; his usual attributes are the lily and the crucifix. In some early works (Sienese school) he holds in his hand a flame, the symbol of his ardent piety. He stands next to St. Francis in the hierarchy of the Franciscans.

Anthony performed many miracles. He is patron of the poor and of barren and pregnant women, and of travelers. He is also invoked for the recovery of lost articles.

Cat. No. S-50—Fig. 81.   ST. ANTHONY.   Detail of Fig. 80.

S-51. ST. FRANCIS

Though relatively small and somewhat crude in its detail, this little figure is remarkably expressive. Francis is depicted as striding forward, his capuche over the head, the cape (here long and reaching almost to the knees), full and wide, as is the robe which reaches to just above the ankles.

The hands, held in front but not crossed, bear the stigmata as do the feet. The face and head are simply carved in strong planes. Only a small portion of the rich brown, tonsured hair shows. He has a small dark moustache and a short beard. The mouth is partly open; the eyes have a sorrowful expression enhanced by the heavily painted lines of the lashes on both lids. All the details are sensitively, though not delicately cut, and withal there is an almost archaic simplicity and directness. The general facial expression is somewhat after the

Cat. No. S-51—Fig. 82.   ST. FRANCIS.
Polychromed wood. 13".

manner of the Spanish painter, Luis de Morales, with its spirited emotionalism, and also some of the qualities of El Greco, without the latter's extreme distortion.

The figure is attached to an irregularly shaped, lozenged base, and between the feet there is a hole for a peg to hold it in place.

Unlike the St. Anthony, (No. S-50), the colors here are dull, lacking the enamel-like luster of the other. Nor is there the "naturalistic" bloom of the flesh tints, for there is but one flat tone.

This small statue is mentioned in the Mission inventory of 1856.

S-52. ST. ANTHONY

This small, polychromed wood statuette represents St. Anthony preaching. It is an extremely simple piece of carving, the body almost columnar, the two arms rather stiffly extended from the elbows. The head is very doll-like and emerges from the simplified collar in an alert and spontaneous manner. The appearance of the face is unlike that of the other sculptures, for here there is an almost amused expression. The color is good; the flesh tones are realistically handled. The color of the habit is a dark blue.

There is no history of this small statue.

Cat. No. S-52—
Fig. 83. ST. ANTHONY.
Polychromed wood. 10".

Cat. No. S-53—
Fig. 84. CARVED CLOCK CASE.
Carved wood and glass. 16".

S-53. CARVED CLOCK CASE

This is an elaborately carved wooden showpiece, formerly used as a clock case, some sixteen inches square at the base and about the same in height, with a heavy beveled glass window, the frame of which is carved in volutes and scrolls.

The case is surmounted by a slightly dome-shaped ceiling, having carved "ribs" extending downward to the corners in the form of pillars, at the bottoms of which are imitation stone urns with flowers. The top is crowned by a scantily dressed full-length figure of ancient Father Time, who has large wings and carries a long scythe; his right foot rests on a globe. At his feet are six cupids in various poses, each of which holds, or has by him, a skull. Each skull by the cupids is different. One is of a soldier wearing a helmet, and the cupid sits on a cannon; another is that of a crowned king. The third skull is that of common man, having no attributes. The fourth cupid has the skull of a pope with tiara.

The two sides have open work with trellised niches. The figures resting in the left niche are missing; those on the right represent two nude children. It is one of those charming genre groups that were characteristic of seventeenth- and eighteenth-century Europe, immortalized in pottery and china as well.

This clock case with the irregular medallions, the shell-like rotunda over the side niches, the broken, recurrent swing of the downward lines, the irregular leaf and scrolls on the front frames are all characteristic of the Baroque. The case now contains a "nativity" scene. There is a tiny doll to represent the Christ Child, other figures, and crudely modeled small animals. The wood carving is superb; it probably orginated in southern Germany or in Austria.

There are no records of the source or acquisition of this piece.

S-54. THE BISHOP'S DOLL

This little bisque doll was called the Bishop's doll, and no explanation was given for his bringing it to the Mission, unless it had been planned for one of the Christmas Nativity scenes.

The figure is some eighteen inches long, fully clothed in satins and white lace, and has Franciscan sandals on its feet. It wears a

Cat. No. S-54—
Fig. 85. THE BISHOP'S "DOLL."
Bisque. 18".

meaningless silk skull cap and there is one small silver bell sewn to the cap and another attached to a cord around the right wrist. This is a rather chubby, satisfied, well-fed infant, with a complacent, mature face with its fine almost acquiline nose, and delicately arched brows. There are traces of eyelashes. The eyes stare upward.

The figure is now "seated" in a small chair with an embroidery and lace pillow at its back and a white satin one for its feet. The hands (of which the left has lost its middle finger) are placed on the chest much in the manner of a child playing.

There is no record of any sort, but it must have been acquired during the residence of the Bishop (1842-1846).

S-55. SMALL CRUCIFIX

This small Crucifix is unquestionably an old piece. The style, which represents the Christ with head inclined downward, is in the tradition and possibly the school of the Spaniard, Martínez Montañés. Yet in spite of the intensely realistic treatment characteristic of this type, there is an unmistakable Gothic quality to the work. The anatomy is excellently handled; it is an almost classical body; the feet, however, are crossed and affixed with one nail. The gathered drapery which covers the loins ends in a typically Baroque flourish, and the slight swing of the body are still further indications of the typically Mexican fusion of earlier Spanish styles.

The Corpus is very battered, and the left arm is entirely missing. All the details of the carving are excellently done, and in spite of its

Cat. No. S-55—
Fig. 86.   CRUCIFIX.
Polychromed wood. 12".

small size, there is a monumental quality about it. True to the Spanish tradition, the desire for extreme naturalism can be seen in the pearly flesh tones of the *encarnación,* in the stream of blood gushing from the wound in the side, and, on the back, the terrible lacerations.

The cross is a good example of the retention of early craftsmanship. Along the arms of the cross, and above and below the Corpus, there are small pieces of brass affixed to the wood. These vary in their designs, but are a derivation in relief (*repoussé*) of Renaissance motifs. In very early crosses of this type the instruments of the Passion were commonly painted on the spare areas of the wood. Here the areas are merely decorative. The piece which was originally above the head of Christ is missing.

S-56. ST. MICHAEL

This representation of St. Michael is of polychromed wood, about 54 inches high, on a 7½ inch base.

The figure stands with his right hand raised almost above his head, the thumb and finger touching; the left hand is extended forward and downward. He wears a round-necked, short-sleeved, knee-length tunic of white on which are elaborate designs of leaves, flowers, and tendrils in gold, blue, and red.

Like most angels in Mission painting or sculpture of this type, he wears boots which are blue with a white design on a band down the front and a gather along the top. There is a long, irregularly draped cloak worn under the tunic, the facing of which is red; the outside is black with a gold-band border. There is also a belt, and a ribbon crossed and tied on the chest. The face is flat, almost expressionless, but well modeled and painted. The flesh is colored pink, the lips red, with blue eyes, brown eyebrows and hair. It is a typical Baroque figure.

The piece is cracked and damaged in the face and right elbow, and the right hand has been burned. The paint is chipping off here and there.

This, and the companion piece, are mentioned in the inventory of 1858.

Cat. No. S-56—
Fig. 87. ST. MICHAEL.
Polychromed wood. 54".

Cat. No. S-57—
Fig. 88. ST. GABRIEL.
Polychromed wood. 54".

S-57. ST. GABRIEL

This polychromed wood sculpture is the companion piece to St. Michael, Figure 87. It has a little more movement with the left hand raised and forward, the head turned up. He wears an undergarment and tunic similar to the other "angel," but with a square-cut neck;

but he, however, has a cuirass of dark blue covering his chest and abdomen. On this are painted leaves and stars, the sun on his right side and the crescent moon with a man's profile on his left. He also wears boots which are golden with dark designs painted on them. His close-fitting cap has jewels painted on the border. The fingers of both hands are broken off. The right hand at one time clasped either a standard or a tall spear.

The eyes in this figure are of glass or china, the pupils of which are dark brown.

S-58. THE FIRST MISSION ALTAR AND TABERNACLE

Important only for its history, this altar has nevertheless some interesting features. The carving and decoration of the tabernacle are the work of Indians, and a more naive presentation of symbols can rarely be found. On each side of the tabernacle door are pieces of mirror set into the wood. Their purpose seems to have been to reflect more light from the altar candles, and also to allow the officiating priest the better to watch the sometimes restless flock behind him.

It is the pediment of the Tabernacle that is most curious. Shaped somewhat in the nature of a wide Bishop's miter, it is of plaster-covered wood, thinly painted in white and pink. For the decorative theme it has all the instruments of the Passion. The center is dominated by a cross about ten inches high, covered with pieces of iridescent abalone shell glued to the surface. Though this use of abalone inset was probably a survival of a decorative device used by the Indians of the Channel areas in decorating many of their articles, it is possible also that it was a copying of a tradition from Mexico, where frames of paintings were often elaborately inlaid with pearl and other substances. On this cross is engraved in lines the figure of the Crucified Christ; the spacing is remarkable in that the arms of Christ are in the arms of the Cross. Below the feet of Christ is the Sorrowful Mother. A "cloth" made of carved wood, hangs from one end of the crosspiece to the other; it was originally painted white. The fineness and simplicity of this crucifix calls to mind the elaborate painted and enameled Florentine crucifixes of the thirteenth century. Even the pose of the Christ is similar; quite possibly the design was copied from a woodcut illustration in a breviary or a missal.

Cat. No. S-58—Fig. 89. THE FIRST MISSION ALTAR.
Painted and inlaid wood.

Cat. No. S-58—Fig. 90. THE "INDIAN" TABERNACLE.
Detail of Fig. 89. 42x40.

The remaining ornament is very crude. On each side of the cross are "diamonds" of abalone shell, two above and two below on each side, and then a wood relief of the Sacred Heart on the left, wrapped in a crown of real thorns, and the Immaculate Heart on the right. To the left of the Sacred Heart is a relief that resembles a jar or receptacle, and opposite is a relief of a vessel. At the extreme left and right respectively are the scourge held by a hand, and another carving representing probably the hand holding the bag with the thirty pieces of silver.

The frame of the pediment is made up of ribbon or scroll-like forms painted blue.

This altar and its tabernacle date from 1789.

S-59. CLASSICAL TABERNACLE

This Tabernacle is of most unusual design, combining several styles. It is an irregular rectangle in shape, and originally must have belonged to a very elaborate altar. It combines classic columns and running cornices with baroque sculptured details. The principal face of the Tabernacle is framed by columns which are repeated on the sides, the basic shape being hexagonal. The door is arched and framed with relief carving. In the center of the door also in relief, is a chalice, above which is a radiant Host. The most arresting feature is the head of an angel that projects from the center of the space above the arched door. Gilded wings sprout from the base of this head.

Cat. No. S-59—

Fig. 91. CLASSICAL STYLE TABERNACLE. Carved, polychromed, and gilded wood. 21x27x18.

The Tabernacle is made entirely of wood, richly polychromed, with much gilt.

60. ST. BARBARA

This is a well-painted, very realistic portrait study of St. Barbara by Domenichino Zampiere, an Italian painter. It is a three-quarter

Cat. No. 60—
Fig. 92. ST. BARBARA.
Oil on canvas. 28x37.

study. She wears a spiked iron crown and carries a long, unsheathed sword in the crook of her left arm. The painting is technically excellent. The forms are well modeled, though lacking in sound construction, and the coloring is easy.

The painting has a curiously sensual quality. Though technically superior to many works at the Mission, it lacks the naive quality and simplicity which lifted the others into the realm of creative painting. Though in no sense similar, the features are very much derived from the type Madonna which Murillo painted in his Conceptions. Here, however, the edges are harder, the coloring more decorative. The subject lacks any spiritual quality.

This painting was given to the Mission in 1946 by Andrew McConnell of Hollywood.

61. ST. FRANCIS

This nearly life-sized oil painting of St. Francis shows him standing on clouds, his head almost at the very top of the canvas. The arms, folded across the breast, support the long crucifix which rests on the right shoulder. His head is turned slightly to the left with the look upward and outward. He wears a light-brown robe, the rough texture of which is indicated by the pattern of very narrow diagonal stripes in black or dark brown on the cloth.

The head is beautifully painted, with strong modeling and a fine understanding of structure. The color is good. The expression is sensitive without being sentimental. This might be an original Spanish work, and is perhaps the best painting of St. Francis in the Mission collection. It belongs to the realistic school of Ribera in Spain and of Páez and Leal in Mexico.

The canvas is badly damaged with a large, crudely repaired tear in the upper right corner, and a bad tear or fold across the lower third of the canvas. This is a companion piece to the Sts. Bonaventure and Anthony in the Choir.

A painting of St. Francis is mentioned in the Mission invoices of 1835, 1854, and 1858, but it is not clear that this is the one.

Cat. No. 61—Fig. 93. ST. FRANCIS. Oil on canvas. 31x61.

62. THE HOLY TRINITY

This small oil on canvas is a remarkably beautiful piece. The painting presents the two large figures of Christ the Son, on the left of the center, and on the right, God the Father. Between them is a large globe on which is a small cross. The globe is banded crosswise. Below them, more or less in the clouds, are the heads of three small child angels with short wings, arranged in the form of a triangle. Directly above, and in the center is the hovering Dove—the Holy Spirit— surrounded by an effulgence of golden rays.

Christ, seated, has His left hand on the globe, His right hand raised before Him with the thumb and middle finger touching; the head is turned slightly to the left and looks out of the picture. He is clothed in a dark red gown; the feet are bare; the long hair is a rich dark brown. He has a dark blue cloak partly about Him. The face is youthful, dignified, kindly.

Opposite to Him is God the Father, a venerable, kindly old man, with white hair and beard, looking in the same direction as the Son; He is clothed almost entirely in the wrappings of His dark green cloak.

Cat. No. 62—Fig. 94. THE HOLY TRINITY.
Oil on canvas. 15x19.

Cat. No. 62—Fig. 95. GOD THE FATHER.
Detail of Fig. 94.

His right hand rests on the globe; in the crook of His left arm is a short staff, or scepter.

Both figures have identical halos: a circle with an inscribed cross. The background is painted a flat gold color, suggesting its Byzantine origin; the dove, in grey blue, is within a triangle. The clouds below are white; the angels, though crudely painted, are realistic in style.

Though this is probably a seventeenth-century Spanish or Mexican work, it could possibly be an earlier work of Italian origin. Whoever the artist was, he was influenced by the style and the externalities of early Florentine or Tuscan work. Yet it has some characteristics of the Mexican school. This is noted particularly in the raised sunburst-like rays emanating from the Dove, and the small angels, but evidences of late Byzantine influence are strong in the gold-brown ground, the thumb and forefinger of Christ and the nimbus.

It is painted on gesso on canvas, both in tempera and oils. There is a heavy impasto to the extent of a sculptural modeling of Christ and the Father, making for relief-like character. There is evidence of successive underpainting and glazes, especially in the robes of Christ and the Father.

It appears as though a later superimposition of heavy white with blue had been used for the angels' wings. The faces and hands of the angels are not of the same style as the heads of Christ and the Father; they look suspiciously like later additions; however, the positions of the wings, sketchy as they are, do suggest the early Florentine style. The total color effect is very rich, simple, and dignified, achieving in its very small compass a sense of largeness.

Traces of varnish or gloss remain. It is an extraordinarily luminous canvas and needs careful restoration and remounting, for it is cracked and torn.

There is no record of this painting.

S-63. WOMAN SAINT OR ANGEL

A most unusual piece, this carved redwood figure is covered with gesso and painted. The head is very small. The figure has its right arm raised, (the lower arm is missing); the left is crooked so that the hand is at the waist. It wears a long full cloak that is of course, woven material covered with thick gesso and then painted pink, white, and gold. The "cuirass" or bodice is likewise of "cloth" and extends to the waist. The close fitting headdress is similarly treated.

The head is sculpturally superior and is best preserved; it could very well have been made separately. Actually where the covering paint is gone, there is evidence of white plaster on the neck. The head resembles a Roman or Greek head rather than a Spanish or Mexican.

Cat. No. S-63—
Fig. 96. WOMAN SAINT OR ANGEL.
Polychromed wood. 14".

The dress or robe is black with gold designs on it, and most of the color and ornament has disappeared.

In spite of a heavy and rather archaic, bulky look, this fragment of some saint or angel has qualities typical of the Baroque sculpture of Mexico. It is possibly a figure of St. Barbara.

There is no history of this piece.

S-64. FAITH, HOPE, CHARITY

These sandstone fragments are all that remain of the three figures that originally had their place on the pediment of the Mission. They fell to the pavement during the disastrous earthquake of June 29, 1925. Cut from native sandstone by the Indians under the supervision of an expert stone carver, they are a mixture of classical and Baroque postures and ideals, and of technical crudity. The understanding of some

Cat. No. S-64—Fig. 97.   FAITH, HOPE, CHARITY.
Carved sandstone.   50".

Cat. No. S-64—Fig. 98. CHARITY. Detail of Fig. 97.

of the truly sculptural problems involved suggests that not only the cutting and execution of these figures, but their design and grouping were under the direction of an experienced sculptor.

The most intact of these figures is the standing one, probably Hope. The arms, which originally were separately carved and then cemented into the sockets, are missing. The head is characteristically archaic: the stiff, set half-smile, the conventionalized hair are reminiscent of both early Greek and early Gothic sculpture for their awkward straightforwardness. The tunic of the figure is Greek in style, rather than in that of the seventeenth century.

The remains of the figure of Faith, with its right hand over the heart, is more in the nature of a relief. The top of the head is gone, as is the lower left arm, where evidence of a fastening bolt remains. The lower portion, which contains the crudely carved feet, is in several fragments.

What remains of Charity are the two lower sections, the most interesting being the trunk. Here a robed woman holds an infant close in her left arm. The infant is "cuddling," the features, though crude, are a good example of the attempt at feeling which was presented. The lower portion of the sculpture is the draped legs, the fluttering robe with the suggestion of some movement in the figure, unlike that of the central figure. It is vaguely reminiscent of the lower drapery of the Nike of Samothrace. The central figure is a little under five feet in height; each of the others vary from three to four feet. There are slight traces of coloring, which would indicate that the imitation of antique sculpture was carried out to the logical extreme.

S-65. STANDING FIGURES

This statue is one of two standing figures that are almost identical in pose, garments, coloring, and expression. They are of polychromed wood, and like the figures in the painting of the Archangels (Figure 57) these are Baroque types. Neither carries any attributes. Each stands on a wooden base 7½ inches tall.

Cat. No. S-65—
Fig. 99. STANDING FIGURE.
Polychromed wood. 48".

Both wear a short white tunic over which is a dark blue Roman-fringed "cuirass" edged and belted in gold. Each has a dark red cloak and wears a small hat, not unlike the helmet of Mercury in Greek pictography. One has a red plume, the other a white plume on his helmet. Each has shoulder-length, curly, brown hair. Both wear the classic boot, open toed, with gold trim and a painted "jewel," gathering the folds of material at the top.

Who these figures are is not clear. They may have been "guardian" figures. They had originally been affixed to a wall, for evidence of a board can be found at the back of each. There is very good workmanship in the carving, but, as is the case in much Baroque sculpture, the underlying structure of the heads and often of the arms is barely suggested. The result is frequently a pudgy, rounded work that, though satisfactory in a general sense, leaves much to be desired for its lack of character. They are probably Mexican in origin.

66. MISSION SANTA BARBARA AND SEMINARY

This quaint oil painting of the Mission is interesting because it is one of the earliest views of the buildings and St. Anthony's Seminary as seen from the slope of the hill to the east. Quite obviously it was painted by a rank amateur; it is in one sense a genuine "primitive." The entire painting is unorganized; there is no sense of scale or perspective, and the buildings, though factually stated, are very much out of drawing. The distant hills are painted as though being directly behind the Mission. The coloring, however, is good; the artist had an observation of color that was far superior to his drawing, and the whole has a certain freshness. It is of some historical value in that it presents certain features of the compound, such as the remains of the major-domo's house, the stone walls and fences, the cisterns, etc., as they existed in 1893.

Cat. No. 66—Fig. 100. MISSION SANTA BARBARA AND SEMINARY.
Oil on canvas. 41x32.

S-67. *MATER DOLOROSA*

This lovely polychromed wood statue is now on a private altar in the Mission. The Virgin stands with weight on the right foot, her hands clasped together almost over her heart. A sharp dirk is imbedded in the breast just above the heart. The knife is a modern, silver-handled piece.

The remarkably expressive face looks upward in resignation. Her head is enframed in a white veil. She wears a dark red dress with a (restored) gold design crudely stenciled on it, a broad yellow shawl-like collar and a rich blue and gold-studded mantle gathered about her. The head was formerly framed in a series of gilded shafts. The colors are quite bright and have been considerably restored, especially on the face and hands. The original variability of the flesh tints has been lost.

This work, although simply executed, without too much detail, is typical of the devotional sculpture of the early eighteenth century, which in Mexico, became increasingly sentimental and dramatic.

The statue is mentioned in the Mexican invoice of February 12, 1801, and arrived at the Mission on December 31 of that year. It is mentioned in the inventories of 1835, 1855, and 1858.

Cat. No. S-67—Fig. 101. *MATER DOLOROSA.*
Polychromed wood. 39".

68. VIRGIN AND CHILD WITH SAINTS

This oil on canvas is in excellent condition and is one of the better works in the Mission. It is very well painted and rich in color harmonies.

Mary, as Queen of Heaven, wearing an elaborate open-work gold crown with a halo of white stars, is seated. On her right knee is the

Cat. No. 68—Fig. 102. THE VIRGIN AND CHILD WITH SAINTS.
Oil on canvas. 31x39.

Infant Jesus, blessing the Souls in Purgatory below.   The Child has a
heavy crown and is nude save for a light white scarf around His waist.
The Virgin's robe is brown; her mantle, rich blue on the inside and
white and gold brocade on the outside, is held up outspread (as a protecting mantle) by St. Joseph in the upper left and St. Teresa on the
upper right.   Joseph has a staff with blossoming lilies.   St. Teresa
wears the habit of a nun, white with black hood and sleeves.   These
four figures dominate the upper part of the canvas.

Below these figures, arranged in the form of a crescent, are the
souls of those who are being helped through the protection of the Virgin
and the Scapular, by two small angels (*putti*) holding scapulars.   On
each side of them, in attitudes of adoration, are two large figures in
thin white robes.

Below the *putti* and other small angels are the Souls in Purgatory.
The colors here are warmer, browner.   Most of the figures are depicted
from the waist up, some in attitudes of supplication, others in prayer.

This is a well-knit composition.   There is a downward curve of
the three heads at the top, centering in the Virgin.   Her face, which
looks outward from the canvas, is sweet and gentle; it is the apex of a
double triangle formed on the outside by the lines of the large figures
in white, and more indirectly, by the lines along the backs of the two
infant angels carrying the scapular.   Actually the convergence of these
two latter lines carries the eye to the Christ Child.   At the very bottom,
in Purgatory, two figures have their arms raised in supplication, and the
extension of these two lines carries the eye upward to the Virgin.

The most dramatic feature of the composition is the shrewd use of
the large dark shadowy area of the gown and mantle in the center of
the canvas, serving to bring into sharp contrast the figure of the Infant
(whose chubby right leg cuts into the dark of the robe), which not only
prevents a sharp division of the canvas, but helps to focus attention.
There is not nearly as much contrast in the lower half of the canvas.
The composition is characteristically two-dimensional, the figures being
essentially on one plane.   Unfortunately, the figures are rather postured, and the expressions on the faces, especially of the Virgin, are
rather wooden.   Nevertheless it is a richly textured painting.

The color distribution is equally good.   The flesh tones of the
figures in Purgatory and of the small angels lead the eye upward to the
cooler tones of the Infant and the face of the Virgin.   The color is

Cat. No. 68—Fig. 103. THE VIRGIN AND CHILD.
Detail of Fig. 102.

subtly varied; one fairly bright red in St. Joseph's sleeve is repeated only
as a warm tone elsewhere. The very deep blue of the mantle is almost
as black as the hood on St. Teresa. This is repeated in the silvery and
lighter blues and blue-greens and greys in the shadows of the figures
and the clouds behind.

The painting came to the Mission in 1941 as a gift from Mr.
Albert Falvey, who procured it in South America. It is a product of
one of the seventeenth-century Mexican schools or studios, very possibly
from the studio, if not the hand, of Cabrera.

Paintings of the Madonna of the Cape, or Cloak, the *Mater Om-
nium* sponsored by the Mendicant Orders, was a common subject, with
variations, especially in France during the fifteenth and sixteenth centuries. She was sometimes alone, sometimes with the Infant Jesus,
sometimes honored by the Trinity and attending angels and saints,

covering all classes of people with her mantle "protecting a devout family." An altarpiece by Jean Miraillet (1425) has her standing, with a multitude under her cloak.

St. Teresa of Avila (1515-1582) was founder of the Carmelite Order of Nuns. She was favored with extraordinary graces and visions, and was one of the great mystics of the Church. Her writings have been compared to those of St. Augustine. She was canonized in 1622.

69. ST. MICHAEL AND THE HOLY TRINITY

This Mexican work is an oil on canvas; it has been badly torn and chipped, although it has been rebacked in part. Much of the paint is gone, and the ground can be seen as a vermillion.

St. Michael wears a blue and white tunic and star-studded bodice, open-toed boots of blue trimmed with white. The wings are blue and blue-white. The flowing, fluttering scarf is bright cadmium red, with the red extending on each side of the figure. He holds a long staff with a cross on top in his right hand. He wears no helmet and the face is turned upward.

Directly above the head of St. Michael is the Trinity. The three figures are all the same size and their heads are almost on a line and very nearly equidistant. The head of Michael and that of the Holy Spirit on the right and Christ on the left, form an equilateral triangle.

Christ at the left leans slightly back, eyes looking out at the observer, with His right hand extended toward the center. In the center is God the Father, His right hand raised, His left resting on a blue sphere and holding a thin cross. The Sacred Heart with a dim ray is exposed. The right-hand figure is the personification of the Holy Spirit with the Dove on the breast. All the faces are very much alike, and it is impossible to tell whether they had been bearded, for the paint has worn off and the scarlet-vermillion underpainting is revealed. The Father is robed in blue, the Son in white, and the Holy Spirit in a pinkish-white.

This is a fairly good work. The rest of the canvas is clouds, with a few angel's heads showing through in four corners. The treatment, especially of the Trinity, is similar but inferior to the Trinity in the large Assumption in the church.

There is no record of this work at the Mission.

Cat. No. 69—

Fig. 104. ST. MICHAEL AND THE
HOLY TRINITY. Oil on canvas. 19x24.

Cat. No. 70—

Fig. 105. ST. FRANCIS IN PRAYER.
Oil on canvas. 45x57.

70. ST. FRANCIS IN PRAYER

This large canvas is a very good work. It was badly damaged in the 1925 earthquake and was heavily restored in August, 1925, by T. N. Lukets.

The painting represents St. Francis kneeling in prayer, facing to the left, before a crucifix in the upper left corner. Before him on a large rock are an open book and a skull. The crucifix stands almost in the shadows. The figure of St. Francis, with hands folded over each other (not clasped or touching in the conventional manner) fills almost the entire center of the painting. Behind and below him, on the right of the canvas is a landscape. Nearest is a small church with bell tower, with pine trees behind it, and beyond, a landscape of rough mountains with the ruins of temples. There is very sharp definition here of dark and light, the most distant lands being painted in a range from white to blue-green. The foliage of the tree behind St. Francis is in the feathery style of the late seventeenth-century Flemish and Italian.

The entire foreground is almost indistinct shadows, with the robe of St. Francis appearing through the shadows. This robe is a light olive-brown with a distinct rough texture of light and dark, so strongly lined that it looks almost like a diagonal pattern.   It is obviously a very heavy, coarse material.

The head is strongly modeled, with a fine strong nose, deep-set eyes and prominent cheek bones, all of which are highlighted.   It is very much in the style of Ribera, a fine face, full of character and emotion and lacking the sentimentalism of Murillo.   The whole is very simply handled.   However, Murillo painted several St. Francis canvases in which the pose is similar to this.   The general character of the work also suggests Valdés Leal, Spanish painter (1630-1691), who was one of the most original exponents of painting in his time.   While he partly imitated Murillo, a strongly personal style is revealed in the greater movement and feeling of restlessness in his work.   His St. Jerome in Seville has somewhat similar qualities to this St. Francis.

Curtis in his catalogue lists (p. 238) under Murillo's works: "300 b— Antwerp Cathedral: St. Francis of Assisi, turned to our left, kneels in a rocky landscape, with his hands clasped before his breast, and looks up to a glory above.   A cross and skull on the ground in front.   Full length.   About 60 by 48 inches."   From this description it is evident that the painter of the Mission St. Francis took the idea, if he did not copy the work, from the Antwerp Murillo.

The canvas is improperly restored.   Blisters are forming here and there where the original canvas is separating from the new backing. It needs thorough cleaning of dulled varnishes.

This painting was given to the Mission in 1920 by a Mr. Johnson of San Francisco.

71. ST. ANTHONY AND THE CHRIST CHILD

This small tempera and oil of St. Anthony is a Byzantine style work painted on a piece of pine about three-quarters of an inch thick. The back of it has remnants of plaster.   The piece is badly warped and the picture is now convex.

The painting represents the barefoot St. Anthony, standing, holding in his right hand a sheaf of three lilies and in his left an open book on which stands the Christ Child clad in diaper and short red cape. The robe is olive-brown; the cowl comes half way down the chest.   The cord has three knots, one at the center of the waist, another half way down, and a third at the bottom. The head, bared and tonsured, is slightly turned to the side.

He stands by a green cloth-covered table on which is a red bound book, both of which are characteristically lacking in accuracy of drawing. The figure is framed by brown curtains, which are gathered by a band about half way down. The background is gold-leaf, much of which is discolored. The floor is a flat, salmon pink. The flesh tones are good.

It is painted on a plaster or gesso ground. There are some incised lines, as in the joined perfect circle halo around the Saint's head, and the enclosed cross halo of the Christ Child.

Cat. No. 71—
Fig. 106. ST. ANTHONY AND THE CHRIST CHILD. Oil on canvas. 45x57.

Cat. No. 71—Fig. 107. ST. ANTHONY. Detail of Fig. 106.

An inscription in red above the halo of St. Anthony has been almost obliterated.   There are three Greek letters LXC almost directly above the head of the Christ Child.   The figure of the Christ Child is a characteristic small Roman man, with well-developed chest and abdominal muscles, and a very mature face; it is hardly the figure of an infant.

The whole is typically late Byzantine in style, possibly early Florentine or Tuscan, yet with considerable shading in the heads and modeling in the fingers and wrists of the hands.   It is purely decorative composition into which the humanism of the Renaissance has been infused, especially in the head of Anthony.

72. CORONATION OF THE VIRGIN WITH THE HOLY TRINITY

This small painting on copper is a very fine work.   The central figure is the Virgin standing on a crescent, her great robe overlapping the heads of two child angels, a serpent and the blue globe below, at the very bottom of the canvas.

The figure is obviously derived from any one of the Murillo Assumptions or Conceptions.   Here, the Virgin looks straight out, her hands closed in prayer and turned to her right.   She is robed in a white gown, with rose-colored bands across the chest; the fluttering cloak or mantle is blue.   The hair is golden brown and falls loosely over the shoulders, and she wears a jeweled crown with other ornaments.   There is a halo of twelve white stars.

Behind her, to each side and in back is the Holy Trinity.   To the center, and above, the Father, in white, with hands raised in blessing, His hair and beard golden brown.   The Sacred Heart, in pink, with a face on it, is seen on the robe through the basket of the Virgin's crown. (This seems oddly out of key and out of place, and might possibly be a later addition.)

To the left is the Son, resembling the Father in appearance, also in white, and with the image of the Lamb on His chest, and the body wound seen through His garment.   The wounds show on the hands and feet.   To the right is the Holy Ghost, with hands crossed at the chest, and the white dove above them.

Below the Virgin, at the left, is a small angel holding a dark blue rectangular bowl for catching the drops of Precious Blood; his head is turned to look at Mary.   In the lower right-hand corner, an angel holds up a gilt-framed ostensorium or mirror.   The serpent of Evil is under foot.

Cat. No. 72—Fig. 108. CORONATION OF THE VIRGIN.
Oil on copper. 12x15.

This is very likely a late seventeenth-century work, similar in style to the large Assumption in the church. It is a fairly good painting and, for the most part, carefully done. There is a consistent grey-blue-green background and pervading tonality. It is typical of the religious painting of the period and has little plastic organization, though the composition is well knit. The expressions on the faces are thoughtfully and carefully executed, and an almost sentimental spirit of kindly benevolence is evident, especially in the Trinity. In contrast, the face of the Virgin is rather expressionless. The four angels at the bottom are much more crudely painted. The rather general inconsistency in technique suggests that the work is a product of a studio, where a master painter develops and finishes the principal subjects and assigns to apprentices the completion or execution of minor parts.

The painting was brought to the Mission by Father Alban in 1922 from Mexico.

73. CHRIST CROWNED WITH THORNS

This work, a very good Italian piece, is by one of the followers of the school of da Vinci, possibly by Cesare de Sesto or Marco D'Oggione. It is an excellent example of the superior realism and the strong chiaroscuro of the style. The medium is a combination of tempera on gesso ground on a wood panel, with very fine and transparent oil glazes. There is no cradling of the wood panel. The principal colors are the ivory-like flesh tones of the face, chest, and hands, and the dark browns of the robe, the rope, and the darker background.

Christ is presented in a three-quarter-length pose, well placed on the panel, with His head bowed in resigned suffering, and His hands crossed. The hands are very well executed and similar in style to those of da Vinci and Luini. The modeling of the head is excellent; the face is expressive without being sentimental. He holds a piece of bamboo staff in His left hand, which is crossed over the right and tied with a heavy cord. The realism is further accented by the drops of blood dripping from the brow and the chest.

The painting was presented to the Mission in June of 1950. It appears to have been restored in places.

Cat. No. 73—
Fig. 109. CHRIST CROWNED WITH THORNS. Oil on canvas. 18x25.

Cat. No. 74—
Fig. 110. OUR LADY OF REFUGE. Oil on canvas. 33x41.

74. OUR LADY OF REFUGE

This subject, presenting the Crowned Madonna and Child, is often known as the *Mater Amabilis.*

The painting is in the general style of the Madonna and Child of the more intimate Italian schools of the sixteenth and seventeenth centuries, with particular Raphaelean influence. The painting, however, is Mexican in character.[14]

The triangular composition presents the Virgin in a three-quarter study, presumably sitting; the lower portions of the body are obscured by clouds. She is clothed in a red gown, with a blue mantle and a golden scarf. The Infant Jesus is half standing before her on a cloud. He is clothed in a very filmy white garment. Both wear elaborate, golden, gem-studded crowns. The Virgin wears drop-pearl earrings and a necklace of large pearls. Several symbolic inscriptions are ingeniously worked into the pattern of the crown, the cloak, and elsewhere.

Though this is a good painting, the poses and expressions are stiff and rather commonplace. It has retained some of the qualities of earlier religious painting but represents the rapid decline into the popular "portrait type" of the near-sentimental religious painting of the nineteenth century. The canvas has some abrasions on the lower left side, and certain retouching is evident.

The painting was brought to the Mission from Mexico by Father Romo in 1882.

The painters of the Madonna rarely varied from established rules set for the colors in which the Virgin-Mother should be clothed, for invariably she wears the red gown or tunic and the blue mantle. The former is the color of love and religious fervor, as well as of the physical, and the latter is the color of constancy and truth as well as the spiritual. The Venetian and German schools frequently presented her in gorgeous and anachronistic clothes. The Christ Child, before the fifteenth century, was always represented fully clothed.

S-75. RELIQUARY BUST OF ST. BARBARA

This curious little polychrome wood bust of St. Barbara is the only piece of its kind in the Mission. Save for broken fingers and chipped paint, it is in good condition. The figure is very probably early seventeenth-century Spanish. The figure has its right arm raised and extended with the position of the fingers suggesting that some article

Cat. No. S-75—Fig. 111. RELIQUARY BUST OF ST. BARBARA.
Polychromed wood. 9".

(probably the Ostensorium) had been held in the hand. The left hand is drawn inward to the waist in front. The figure looks straight ahead.

The face is a large oval, cream-colored with traces of pink; the eyebrows are carefully painted on. The face is framed by heavy dark brown hair. She wears a wreath and a cap. In the center of the forehead at the hair line, there is a small four-petaled flower. She is robed in a heavy gown gathered by a twisted "cord" at the waist, and a beautifully brocaded cape is thrown over her right arm. The gilding of the robe and cloak dominate, though the principal color is dull red. The most unusual feature is the presence of a large medallion 2½ inches high and 2 inches wide on the chest, in the center of which is a glass-covered opening through which one can see what may be a relic of the saint. The figurine is actually a reliquary.

The figure has been riveted to a pedestal three inches high. It was presented to the Mission by Mr. Harry Downie of Carmel on August 6, 1949.

S-76. MADONNA AND CHILD

This small statuette is a South American piece brought to the Mission by Father Patrick Roddy. It is of rather crudely carved wood, covered with gesso and painted. The figurine stands on a broad pedestal, 4½ inches high, also wooden, and of more recent origin. She is dressed in a long, elaborately decorated gown over which there is a cape, made of linen dipped in plaster or gesso and then painted, and now very fragile. The gown is dark cream color with an intricate pattern of red and black, traces of which remain. The collar is undecorated and is

Cat. No. S-76—Fig. 112. MADONNA AND CHILD.
Polychromed wood and cloth. 11″.

Cat. No. S-76—Fig. 113.   MADONNA.   Detail of Fig. 112.

a simple area of gesso or plaster colored a dun brown.   The ornaments on the gown are in relief.[15]

The hands of the figure are close to the body; the left supports the Infant which is separately carved of wood and has an almost primitively carved face.   The hair on both heads is dark brown and treated as a homogenous mass; all the skin showing is a rather mat tan.   The Infant is 3¼ inches long.

At some time or other the figure was clothed in what is now a faded, very old, ivory-colored silk robe and cape edged with cloth and silver lace, and over which was a pale aquamarine blue satin mantle. Most of this is falling to pieces.   Two strands of fine gold beads are hung around the neck, and a crown of gold-washed brass rests on the head.

77. "MEXICAN" MADONNA AND CHILD

This very unusual painting is a good example of Mexican work, possibly painted by an Indian with conisiderable talent. It presents the Virgin with the Christ Child seated in the crook of her left arm. The principal characteristic of this painting is its remarkable Byzantine-like quality of flat decorativeness, although the actual painting and workmanship is in no sense Byzantine. Also interesting is the fact that both the Virgin and Child are painted as Indians with very dark, almost brown skins.

The features are extremely well executed; the face of the Virgin is especially sensitive with luminous eyes. The nose is rather long in each of the figures, and the face of the infant is that of a mature man. A rather flat treatment is used in the rendering of the hands and there is little shading.

Cat. No. 77—Fig. 114. "MEXICAN" MADONNA AND CHILD.
Oil on canvas. 12x16.

The painting is probably an early nineteenth-century work, copied or adapted from a Russian-style work, for the flat, frontal pose, the rather stiff treatment of the gown and the folds of the veil as they fall on each side of the face are very similar to those in Russian icons. The crowns on both heads are likewise somewhat Russian in style, tapering outward to a wider top. The crown in each case appears as a continuation of a wide band that presumably inscribes both heads but is painted up to the sides of the crowns. This halo is painted a chrome yellow which, excepting where it is applied more heavily in the form of pattern lines, has dulled to a murky mustard color.

The coloring, aside from the brown skins is also very un-Mexican. The cloak of the Madonna is a deep Prussian blue-green that has disintegrated in some areas; the lining of this cloak was originally a vermillion color. The edging is a band of chrome yellow with touches of orange, the intent probably being to suggest gold or gilt. The gown proper is a rich green. The robe of the Christ Child is the only typically Mexican feature in the painting. The principal color is a varying pink-red, but over this, painted in rather heavy impasto, are brush strokes of very pale pink and white to suggest the modeling of the arms and legs. These brush strokes are very crude and appear to be later additions to the work, for nowhere else save in the detail of the halos are similar brush strokes found. Also noteworthy is the use of a fluid line to define the forms and the details of the hands and fingers. Similar lines in what appears to be black are used on the edge of the Infant's face, the upper eyelids of the Mother, and in the definition of the edge of the lips.

The pigment has been destroyed in several places, notably in the base coloring of the two crowns and in the area of the red-orange lining of the cloak where the bare canvas shows. It appears as though the pigments had been removed by vigorous cleaning; apparently these base colors had been more fugitive and soluble, for the jeweled details of the crowns, which are in thick dark blue-green, have remained.

This is a handsome decorative painting; a close and rich harmony exists between the dark tones and the warm brown background. It needs a very careful cleaning to remove traces of darkened varnish and shellac in order to restore some of the original brilliance of the piece. Furthermore, it has been clumsily glued to a wooden backing that has cracked, and blisters and wrinkling have appeared on the surface of the canvas from the improper gluing. It is a recent addition to the Mission.

S-78. OUR LADY OF THE ROSARY

This is a full-length sculpture, of wood with gesso and rich polychromy.

The Virgin stands erect, holding the Infant in her left arm with the right extended, holding a rosary in her hand.

She wears a very rich, gold-embroidered dress, a dark blue cloak edged in an embossed gold border of leaves and geometric design, and over her shoulders is a short silver-grey blue shawl. The inside of the cloak is painted brownish. She wears a gold tiara (of metal) of intricate leaf and filigree set with colored stones and rhinestones. This crown is definitely not of the original period. Originally there was a halo, or an effulgence, attached to the back of the head, for there is

Cat. No. S-78—Fig. 115.   OUR LADY OF THE ROSARY.
Polychromed wood. 31".

evidence of some such ornament having been in place at one time. There is similar evidence in the head of the Infant.

The Infant is represented as partly seated, with hands extended. In a sense it is an Infant, yet it retains some of the characteristics of a mannikin. The Infant is separately carved, and has a dowel-like protuberance that fits into the Madonna's hand, so that it will not slip off. The eyes of the Mother and Child are identical, brown, of porcelain, set in doll-like faces. The color of the faces has been restored. The face is beautiful in its sensitivity.

The statue is in good condition, save for evidence that the arms of the Infant had been broken off and simply reattached; the front part of the Infant's left foot is missing, as is part of a finger of the Virgin's left hand.

This is a Mexican piece, probably late seventeenth-century, of considerable merit. There is a grace in the pose that is somewhat reminiscent of the German and Flemish Madonnas. It is simply carved and free from extraneous detail.

This generic type of Madonna, including the *Inmaculadas,* stems almost directly from the works of the Spanish sculptor Martínez Montañés (1568-1649), one of the greatest of his time. The making of devotional figures was one of the chief tasks of the sculptor during this period; he was required to realize all the states, positions, attitudes, and appearances which were connected with the mystical experiences of the saints and the devout in the Spain of his time. Much more indicative of that realization are the sculptures of the Saints and the Crucified Christ; such may be seen in the great Crucifix on the Reredos (Figure 30) and the St. Francis (Figures 124 and 125).

It is mentioned in the Mexican Invoice of March 18, 1806, and in the inventories of the Mission for 1835, 1856, and 1858. Robinson describes it in *Life in California* (1891 edition).

S-79. ST. MICHAEL THE ARCHANGEL

This St. Michael is a very fine example of Mexican Baroque sculpture. The saint is represented as standing firmly on a grotesque creature with a human head and serpent's body, the tail spiraling upward and ending in a spear head. The wings are rather small, reaching about to his temples; his right hand holds a thick, round-bladed sword, and in his left, the scales of judgment. These are modern additions.

He wears a Mercury-like helmet, surrounded by a small cross. The hair is golden brown and wavy. The sensitive face on a rather thick neck looks downward; the eyes are well set in, the nose and mouth well carved. The flesh tones with high color in cheeks, and on the chin and lips, remain.

He is clothed in the seventeenth-century chiton, with short, gathered sleeves, and a pleated knee-length kilt. This was originally gold with an irregular pattern of very dark blue or black "demons." The right side of this has been repaired, and the original color of the kilt is still clearly evident in the back. The inner lining of the sleeves is bright red with gold dots; the outside was probably dark green, for there are traces at the back. The armor, formerly embellished with gold designs, is now almost colorless. A trailing half-skirt at the back, encompassing the legs, is very dark green. He wears open-toed boots that are colored black with gold dots, and a dark red stocking trim.

This is a most appealing statue. The wings are definitely modern additions, for there is no evidence of gesso or underpainting, and furthermore, the blue in back shows. Though almost devoid of color above the knees, it is in excellent condition.

The statue is listed in the Mexican invoice of February 12, 1801, and arrived at the Mission on December 31 of the same year. It is listed in the inventories of 1855 and 1858.

Cat. No. S-79—
Fig. 116. ST. MICHAEL THE ARCH-
ANGEL. Polychromed wood. 30".

Cat. No. S-80—
Fig. 117. THE VIRGIN AND ST.
ILDEFONSO. Polychromed wood.
32x25x8.

S-80. THE VIRGIN AND ST. ILDEFONSO

This polychromed wood carving is an excellent piece, very possibly of Spanish origin, although the features of the Virgin have a strong Indian cast. It is in a sense a relief work, though the figures are almost freestanding. It represents the Virgin in the act of placing the cassock on the kneeling Ildefonso. The group is carved from a single piece of wood by a minor sculptor in a fairly realistic manner. The sculptor had a fine sense of design; the compact character of the group is unified by a strong linear quality that encompasses the figures. The silhouette is extremly simple and unbroken; the details are concentrated in the faces and folds of the garments. There is a rather archaic quality present in the somewhat stiff poses of the two figures.

Coloring is subdued but rich. The brilliance of the original coloring must have been considerable, for over all there is a deep reddish golden glow. Traces of deep reds and dark blue-blacks from a now lost *estofado* pattern remain. The features of both the Virgin and the Saint are excellently modeled and painted with restraint and without naturalistic detail. The background area, with its coarse texture revealing the toolmarks of the sculptor, is a dull gold.

The piece is in a state of good preservation save for a few surface abrasions. It was presented to the Mission by Mr. Albert Falvey in February, 1942.

St. Ildefonso was one of the first Spanish Benedictines. He died in January, 667, after a lifetime of devotion to the Virgin Mary. His great vision was that in his church when the Virgin was seen by him seated on his throne at the high altar. She put over him a cassock of "heavenly substance" and the angels who were her attendants adjusted it. From that time he never occupied the throne nor wore the garment.

81. ST. FRANCIS SOLANUS

This work is a full-length oil on canvas of St. Francis Solanus among the Indians. He stands erect in wooded country, his upraised right hand holding a crucifix, his left down at his side holding a violin and a small sheaf of lilies. He is dressed in a rough grey-blue habit and wears barefoot sandals. This is a well-painted canvas, although the pose and expression are wooden and rather stiff, and the face is almost expressionless, though well modeled. He has a rather haggard and sunken look and an unearthly pallor.

Below and on the left is a scene in miniature showing him baptizing the pagan Indians (of the New World). The two men are clothed only in loin cloths of feathers, while the woman who is holding an infant is fully clothed in blue and white robes. On the other side in the distance are more Indians, one of whom is shooting a bow and arrow. There are hills and trees, the large one on the left has six birds in the act of singing. (One is a bright red-breasted robin.)

The canvas had been cut from its original frame and reglued to a new canvas. The varnish, which has turned yellow-brown, makes a film of tone over the whole; the blue sky and pale orange sunset, the neutral green ground, and the blue-grey hills result in a rather dull painting.

This painting is undoubtedly late eighteenth-century, and by some minor Mexican artist. It is awkward and unconvincing, yet most interesting historically. Stylistically, it belongs to the earlier Italo-Spanish tradition, somewhat suggesting the multiple scene works of the late Gothic period. St. Francis is the principal subject, but his work among the Indians surrounds him.

Cat. No. 81—

Fig. 118.   ST. FRANCIS SOLANUS.

Oil on canvas.   26x35.

The painting is mentioned in the Inventories of 1854 and 1858.

St. Francis Solanus was born in Andalusia, Spain, of distinguished parents. After completing his studies with the Jesuits, he entered the Order of the Friars Minor. Early in his work in the Church, he asked to be sent to foreign missions, and was sent to South America, where he spent twenty years with great success among the Indians. He had a miraculous power in that, through his contact, the Indians became meek and were eager converts. He wrought many miracles even during his lifetime. He died on the feast of St. Bonaventure, 1610.

82. ST. CATHERINE OF ALEXANDRIA

Cat. No. 82—
Fig. 119.   ST. CATHERINE OF
ALEXANDRIA. Oil on canvas. 30x40.

This oil on canvas is obviously a copy of an early nineteenth-century Mexican work, very possibly a so-called Primitive. The saint is presented standing in rich costume: a white gown, blue tunic, and a fur-lined brilliant vermillion cloak. She wears a gold crown and holds a palm in her left hand; her right rests on a long sword. At her left is a broken segment of a torture wheel. Behind her is a cloudy sky, grey and white mountains, and muddy-colored ridges of hills.

The painting is hard, crude, and badly drawn and colored. The expression on the face is conventionally placid. It is typical of the mediocre work turned out by hundreds of "artists" during the last century to satisfy the desire of the pious for religious "art" and is interesting only as a curiosity. The canvas is damaged by tears and is very soiled.

There is no history on this canvas.[16]

St. Catherine of Alexandria, virgin and martyr, was daughter of Sabinella, Queen of Egypt. She was exceedingly wise and, upon the death of her father, became heiress to the kingdom, but became a recluse and refused marriage. She became converted to Christianity after a vision-like dream. She rejected the Emperor Maximin and, through her virtue and resistance to torture, caused the conversion of many pagans. She was tortured and subsequently beheaded, but her body was borne to Mt. Sinai by angels. Catherine is patroness of education, science, philosophy, and of all students, and of eloquence. She is represented as richly dressed. Her attributes are the broken wheel, and she has also the martyr's palm, the crown of royalty, and the book.

83. ST. ANTHONY IN ADORATION

This canvas of St. Anthony is similar to the St. Catherine of Figure 119 in character, but the coloring is not as garish.

The Saint, shown down on his left knee, in profile, is before a table on which is the Gospel. The Christ Child, draped with a pink scarf, stands on the book, looking down, and leans with outstretched arms to the Saint. Above and between them are two young angels' heads with wings observing the vision with pleasure.

The coloring is spotty, and the blue of St. Anthony's habit and the cloth covering the table dominates. The entire background is a muddy brown. Like the St. Catherine, this painting has a primitive quality and may be the work of Indians trained in the art schools of Mexico. The drawing is likewise awkward and stiff.

Cat. No. 83—
Fig. 120. ST. ANTHONY IN ADORATION. Oil on canvas. 29x37.

There is no history of this canvas.

84. MISSION SANTA BARBARA IN 1881

John Sykes painted the Missions as many amateurs did: as literally as he could. The scene is accurate, but the drawing is bad. The coloring is rather hard and sharp, though the distant mountains are quite well done. There is a collection of Sykes' paintings of other missions in the museum rooms.

The scene shows the front of the Mission. The large tower buttress is out of drawing, as is the façade. The little wooden belfry at the extreme end of the *convento* building is sharply indicated, but on the whole the perspective and realization is poor. He also shows on the extreme right the two adjoining tile-roofed buildings (probably those of the major-domo), and as such this is a good record. The Indian *lavandería* and the fountain are conspicuous in the foreground.

Sykes was a Santa Barbara painter and apparently self-trained. The work is signed and dated 1881 in the lower left-hand corner, and opposite is the inscription "Santa Barbara 1786." On the back of the canvas he has painted in outline three skulls and crossbones, and the wording: "Mission S. B. Cal. BY JOHN SYKES 1881." The canvas is in very good condition; it appears to have been restretched.

Cat. No. 84—Fig. 121. MISSION SANTA BARBARA IN 1881.
Oil on canvas. 34x20.

85. MISSION SANTA BARBARA IN 1890

This large canvas of the Mission, unlike the others, is not only superior in drawing and painting, but is a close-up view of the principal aspect: the façade of the church with the fountain directly in the foreground. It is accurate and very well painted; perhaps there is a little too much insistence on the textured quality of the stone surface of the building, which here does not appear to be covered with a coat of stucco. Though a bit hard, the coloring is on the whole very good, and the unknown artist who painted this was a capable one. The textures of the trees, stone, earth, and tile are well contrasted. There is good balance of light and dark; the luminous pebble-clouded sky, with a pattern of cloud shadows on the building, the dust-raising flock of sheep, and the looming towers in an early morning light make this a superior though romantic painting.

Cat. No. 85—Fig. 122. MISSION SANTA BARBARA IN 1890.
Oil on canvas. 40x30.

86. SANTA BARBARA ADOBE

This small work, an extremely well-painted picture of an adobe house, is technically superior to John Sykes' oil paintings of the Missions. It is not dated, but is very probably a much later work than

Cat. No. 86—Fig. 123. SANTA BARBARA ADOBE. Watercolor. 20x8.

Figure 121.   The scene is a ruined adobe on a knoll, with the hills and a view of the coast in the background.   The structure is very nearly in ruins, with but little plaster covering the adobe bricks, and with a dilapidated tile roof.   It could possibly be one of the Mission compound buildings.

Sykes has used his colors well in this small work, with the necessary detail in the building and all else rather broadly suggested.

The painting is a recent gift to the Mission.

Cat. No. S-87—Fig. 124.   ST. FRANCIS WITH
THE CROSS.   Polychromed wood.   60".

S-87. ST. FRANCIS WITH THE CROSS

This very good sculpture is a full-length, almost life-sized figure of St. Francis with the Cross.   It is a late seventeenth-century Mexican work of polychromed wood; it is believed to have originally been at the Santa Cruz Mission.

St. Francis wears the full dark brown habit with a modern cord. The right hand is extended; the left holds the cross at which he is gazing. The feet are bare.

The workmanship is simple and direct, especially good in the modeling of the head, which is very nearly conventionalized. The characteristic Spanish emotionalism is expressed in the rather sorrowful expression of the eyes with their upturned brows and the partly open mouth. The eyes are of porcelain with brown irises. The modeling here is interesting in that the inner corner of the eye is set deeper into the socket than is the outer corner. The nose is prominent with a high and sensitive ridge, and the close-cropped, tonsured hair is almost reduced to a formalized pattern. The hands have the stigmata.

Cat. No. S-87—Fig. 125.   ST. FRANCIS.
Detail of Fig. 124.

The hood and cowl of the habit are rather loose and form almost a circle from which the slender neck arises. The colors of the face and skin, which have been restored in part, are good.

This carving of wood was covered with a layer of gesso and burlap, or linen which had been dipped into the plaster or gesso, and then molded to the carving. The statue is in good condition.

This statue was believed to have been in Santa Cruz as late as 1829. It was received at the Mission here on October 4, 1882.

S-88. CRUCIFIXION GROUP

One of the most interesting sculptures is the Crucifixion group, a fairly large four-figure group, presenting the Crucified Christ with the two Marys and St. John. The Cross, of mahogany, with end decor of brass, is about thirty inches high, with a metal inscription (INRI) above, and is set on a slight rise of piled up "rocks," covered with gesso and plaster, and painted.

The figures at the foot of the Cross are separate and on individual bases. There are curious inconsistencies here, for the execution of all details is very skillful, but the postures are mannered and stilted.

The Corpus on the Cross is very good, a rather lean Christus with His body slightly twisted, and with long thin arms and legs. The arms form a very wide V; the head is tilted to the right and the face turned up. The head is framed in a bright aureole of shafts of gold. The body color is ivory, the scant drapery a little whiter. The legs are almost straight and close together. The nails are headed with bits of glittering clear glass or cut quartz. There are two prominent wounds, one on the chest at the left, the other quite low on the right. There is some color of the blood flowing down the arms. At the base of the cross is a skull and crossbones.

Immediately behind and to the right of the cross is the kneeling Mary Magdalene. She has her right hand curved up and around the cross behind the knees of Christ. She is dressed in a very richly brocaded gold dress with a blue and red cloak around her left shoulder and arm. The feet are in sandals. Two fingers are missing from the delicately

Cat. No. S-88—Fig. 126. **CRUCIFIXION GROUP.** Polychromed wood. 36x60.

carved right hand. The face is turned up in adoration, and is framed by an eight-rayed nimbus.

On the right is St. John the Evangelist standing with the head somewhat thrown back, the right hand over the heart, the left out-stretched. He wears a dark, almost black, long gold-brocaded robe over which is a rich red cloak. He is barefoot. Like the Magdalen, his hair is long and dark. His pose, with the weight thrown back, is rather theatrical. The face is exactly like that of the Magdalen, and it is only the traditional position that makes clear the identity of the figure.

Mary the Mother of Christ is on the left, somewhat forward, and turns in toward the group. She has her left hand on her breast, her right stretched outward and down. She wears a dark veil over her head, a white "collar," a dark red robe and deep blue gown. The feet are shod in dark sandals. She has an eight-rayed halo.

This group appears to be a late seventeenth-century work. It is in good condition save for abrasions and a few missing fingers. It is har-monious in color and unified. The Cross may probably be modern.

Cat. No. S-88—
Fig. 127. CHRIST ON THE CROSS.
Detail of Fig. 126.

There is little evidence of restoration except in the flesh tones on the figure of Mary. The carving of the face of Christ is excellently achieved, the moment before death having been selected by the sculptor. The faces of the Marys, though sensitive and with considerable nobility, are rather mask-like. They are similar to that of the *Mater Dolorosa* (Figure 101) and may have originated in the same studio.

This sculpture group belongs to an altar and was probably designed to be placed above the tabernacle.

There is no history of this group.

89. ST. ANTHONY

This oil on canvas, the companion piece to St. Bonaventure, (Figure 129) is the same size and has similar characteristics. Here the Saint is carrying the Infant Jesus in the crook of his left arm, and steadies Him with his right hand. The Infant holds a single spray of lilies.

Cat. No. 89—
Fig. 128. ST. ANTHONY AND THE INFANT JESUS. Oil on canvas. 31x63.

The Saint is in the light brown-grey which was the color of the early Franciscan habit; the cord has five large knots and one small one at the very end. Like St. Bonaventure, the face is very young, here almost effeminate in its delineations and softness, especially in the orange-red lips and the faint blush on the cheeks. The close-cropped hair is brown.

The Infant is well painted, and very similar to the late type found in some Murillos. He is clothed in a thin, filmy, white tunic, through which the delicate flesh tones can be seen. The head, which is turned and looks down slightly, is cherubic with its rosy, blooming cheeks and fine golden hair.

The painting is good, though it lacks the character of the St. Francis (Figure 93), perhaps because of the fact that the Saint is looking out of the picture away from the Infant, and the Infant's unconcern (for here He is just a lovely baby).

There is a crease about halfway up. It is yellowed from irregular varnish and accumulated dirt.

The painting is mentioned in the Inventory of 1858.

90. ST. BONAVENTURE

This is a full-length figure of St. Bonaventure, holding a large open book in his left hand, resting against the thigh; in his raised

right hand, he holds a grey quill pen. Over his grey-brown habit he wears a scarlet circular cape that reaches almost to the elbows and on his head and a small skull cap of similar color.

The face is that of a young man, a smooth, almost round face that is turned upward. The hair is light brown, the flesh tones clean and fresh. There is an almost youthful quality about the painting. The hands are likewise free of wrinkles.

There is good painting here, with a sense of form and bulk beneath the habit that gives to the figure an almost columnar quality. The setting is open space, a grey-brown ground with white and grey clouds in a blue sky.

Like the St. Francis of Figure 93 and the St. Anthony, Figure 128, the textured habit is so strongly marked that it is almost a striped material.

Cat. No. 90—
Fig. 129. ST. BONAVENTURE.
Oil on canvas. 30x62.

The canvas is in fairly good condition; there is a horizontal crease mark, around which the paint has cracked, almost halfway up the canvas. Otherwise it is in fair condition; parts have been patched up and the whole has a film of yellowed varnish that has gathered in spots.

This painting is listed in the Mission Inventory of 1854, and of 1858.

St. Bonaventure, entitled the "Seraphic Doctor," was one of the greatest writers and teachers of the Church. He was born in Tuscany

(Italy) in 1221. As a child, he became a disciple of St. Francis, became a Franciscan at twenty-seven years, and then went to study theology in Paris. He was distinguished for his humility and for his personal ministry to the poor. He was made general of the Order in 1256, and later was made a cardinal. He died at fifty-three from overwork.

He is represented in many ways, sometimes with a cape over his grey habit, with the Bishop's miter on his head, and the Cardinal's hat hanging from a tree or at his feet. Occasionally, he is attired in the crimson robes and hat of the Cardinal with a book in his hand.

91. ALTAR OF OUR LADY OF REFUGE

An unsigned and undated ink and wash drawing of a large altar, probably made in 1842, is this design for the altar of the projected Cathedral which was to have been built for the first Bishop of the Californias.

Cat. No. 91—
Fig. 130. ALTAR OF OUR LADY OF REFUGE. Ink on paper. 9x14.

The drawing is quite obviously derived from Greco-Roman sources, and very probably from the Vitruvius in the Mission Library. In matters of proportion much is lacking, for the small, rectangular box-like altar itself is completely overshadowed by the immense classical façade of the altar screen. The tabernacle rests on a shelf extending beyond the width of the altar and is actually an opening in the screen. Immediately above the door of the tabernacle is a domed niche, intended probably for the altar crucifix. Above this is a garland. Most prominent on the screen are two pairs of Ionic pilasters, one pair on each side of the center. Above these is the heavy entablature consisting of the architrave, frieze, and cornice. The decorations consist of a rather naive border made up of fishes and garlands and rows of egg-and-dart and guttae patterns. Surmounting this is a round painting of Our Lady of Refuge, which painting is garlanded with leaves and roses. A small urn on each side completes the symmetry. See the Bishop's Tomb, Figure 36.

The drawing is the work of an imaginative though technically untrained person. It is obvious that the façade was copied from some model or models and is quite accurately presented in its perspective and suggestion of modeling. The drawing of the altar itself, however, is woefully inaccurate and is, perhaps, the only original part of the drawing.[17]

It is executed on fairly absorbent paper with a watermark "S & B, N H." The work is partly in pen, in both brown and black ink, as well as in washed tones of grey and black ink. It is stained and torn. The marbleized effect in the drawing is very similar (in its disregard for real marble) to the painted dado in the Church.

92. OUR LADY OF MOUNT CARMEL

This large, lunette-shaped canvas hung for many years with its companion piece, The Last Judgment, on the walls of the Sanctuary. It is now on loan to Mission St. Anthony of Padua.

The painting is a rather spectacular devotional as well as narrative piece. It is almost rigidly symmetrical. There is no dominant color although the lower portion of the canvas is predominantly brownish, in sienna tones. The upper two-thirds is a greyish silver. There is little depth in spite of the figures being well modeled. The head of the Virgin is very much in the style of Murillo, in contrast to the Rubens-like figure of a woman in the lower right-hand corner. There is also an extraordinarily well-painted head of an old man.

The Virgin is seated and holds the Christ Child on a small red cushion in her lap. Her gown is a dark reddish-brown with a gold edging. The mantle is a clear, light blue, with some of the white lining showing. On her head is a very large, somewhat awkward crown of red silk with gold-set pearls. Her face has a sweet, rather weak expression. A halo of small angel heads, in pale flesh and buff colors, surround them. Her feet rest on three richly painted Murillo-type angel heads. In her right hand she holds a scapular with red ribbons and a delicate, carved stick.

Cat. No. 92—Fig. 131. OUR LADY OF MT. CARMEL. Oil on canvas. 170x90.

On each side of the Madonna are two angels. The one to her right is clothed in a star-studded blue gown with a red cloak; the one to her left is in white and yellow with a soft red cloak fluttering behind, leading a small child in a white robe.

In the lower portion of the canvas are the upper parts of seven figures in Purgatory, four men and three women. One, at the extreme left, is probably a friar. The angel on the left is beckoning these souls to heaven; the angel on the right, who has the young child, leads it directly upward.

The painting is badly cracked from folding, with three strong creases that almost bisect it horizontally. The damage to the canvas is considerable, with holes in the hair of the Child Jesus and the wing of the angel. The canvas is very loose, but the pigment is in good condition where it has not worn off.

The technique is consistent throughout, though the style of the figures varies considerably. It is quite apparent that this is the work of a studio, very possibly from the school of Nicolás Rodríguez Juárez.

The painting is mentioned in the Mission inventory of 1835 and again in 1858. It was very popular with visitors to the Mission. Brewer mentions it in his diary of 1861.

93. THE LAST JUDGMENT

This large lunette-shaped canvas has been said to be a copy of a Murillo Last Judgment. Though this is highly improbable, it nevertheless has some characteristics of the school of that artist. Like the Our Lady of Mount Carmel, it hung for a long time in the Sanctuary but is now at Mission St. Anthony of Padua.

The composition is most complex. It is divided into right and left by the figure of Christ, with the Cross below Him. However, the principal division of the canvas is horizontal. In the upper third is a cloud area with Christ in the center (Paradise). The middle section is the Earth in tumult, and the lower third represents Purgatory with the mouth of Hell in the extreme right-hand corner.

Cat. No. 93—Fig. 132.   THE LAST JUDGMENT.   Oil on canvas.   110x90.

In the upper section, the dominant figure is the lightly draped figure of Christ, His wounds showing, half seated on a throne with His feet resting on a blue globe. He is almost nude save for an enveloping scarlet robe across His right arm and wrapped around the waist. His left hand is raised and in it He holds a curved sickle. He is surrounded by a radiance. On each side of Him are bands of angels and the blessed standing on clouds. To the left of Christ, on a higher band of clouds is John the Baptist, and on His right, the Virgin Mary, both in attitudes of adoration. Below the globe is the Book of the Apocalypse opened to Chapter XX. To the right are three large figures, one with a crown; to the left is a pope and a white-robed friar. Below the book is an angel holding the Cross. At the extreme right of the bank of clouds are two prophets with banners bearing inscriptions.

The center area of the canvas is given over to cities of towers, buildings, classical ruins, fortifications, and grottoes. There is great activity here; groups of people are being herded in many directions by angels, each of which is postured in the classical or Baroque manner. The ones on the left are those who are to enter Paradise; their faces are uplifted and the color scheme is lighter and more golden. The Archangel Gabriel separates these from the figures on the right, who are all more contorted. Devils and serpents entwining columns appear. Four persons hang from a gallows atop a domed, temple-like building. There is also a pit into which people are falling.

Superimposed upon the extreme left of this scene is a half-length portrait of the Blessed Virgin Mary wearing a white robe, her hair falling about her shoulders. This figure bears no relation to the large canvas; it is enclosed by a sketchily painted oval frame. It has the appearance of being a later, superimposed painting, for both the style and the expression are completely out of key with the remainder.

Across the lower portion of this canvas are Death, Purgatory, and Hell. The waist-length figure of the skeleton, Death, is wearing a shroud or mantle and stares emptily into space. This figure, like that of the Blessed Virgin above it, is enclosed in a brown oval frame. Most of the rest of the scene below is very dark. Between Death and Purgatory, a nearly nude, classic-style Angel, a white-robed woman seated beside him, turns to observe the sufferings of those who are in Purgatory, where there is a mixture of nude and semi-nude bodies, skeletons, and devils in a cave. At the extreme right is a huge mouth of Hell in which devils with hideous faces work on the condemned. This section recalls the fantastic paintings of Hieronymus Bosch.

This huge painting is perhaps the most interesting of the Mission collection.[18] In it all the teachings and precepts of the Church are presented. It is in a sense a dramatic allegory. The manner of presentation suggests comparisons with other paintings; for example, the Paradise calls to mind the upper portion of Raphael's *Disputà* in the Vatican; the intense activity of the center part, with its superimposed portraits of the Virgin and Death, suggests the return to the Gothic multi-scened paintings, which the very nature of the subject demands. The composition holds together by virtue of the characteristic blue-grey and silvery tonality.

The painting has been restretched. Originally the canvas ended some three inches inward from the present frame or stretcher. Similar evidence is on the opposite side, where the blue-grey pigment terminates abruptly. The canvas is loose and is very dirty. There are several holes and some bad cracks and abrasions along the lower portion.

The painting is listed in the Mission inventories for 1835 and 1858.

S-94. ST. JOSEPH

This polychromed wood statue of St. Joseph is now on loan to Mission St. Anthony of Padua.

The standing St. Joseph wears a black robe decorated with elaborate gilt flowers and leaves, and a mantle or cloak which is dull red inside, and gold with a pattern of blue and red roses on the outside. The right hand is extended and holds the traditional staff with lilies. The feet are in open sandals colored gold with narrow red stripes. The facial color is a very pale flesh tint, with both hair and beard black.

This is an excellently carved Mexican work. The markedly long neck of the Gothic style is retained here, as are the elongated nose and the almost oriental eyes, which here are of porcelain. The gesso and the coloring are gone from the fingers of the left hand, and from several areas on the head. All details are very carefully painted. The wood has cracked and warped; the head is split, and the face may fall off.

The statue is mentioned in the Mission inventory of 1855.

Cat. No. S-94—
Fig. 133. ST. JOSEPH.
Polychromed wood. 48".

Cat. No. 95—
Fig. 134. ST. BARBARA.
Oil on canvas. 22x30.

95. ST. BARBARA

A full-length painting in oil on canvas of this woman saint, probably St. Barbara, belongs to the late eighteenth-century Mexican school. The figure stands in a hilly landscape, now very dull in color but originally a luminous blue-green. The sky is similarly lacking in color.

St. Barbara is dressed in a dark blue-green gown with a deep red underdress. Over this is worn a dark, rather dull red-orange cloak. On her brown hair is a filmy white veil, on top of which she wears a small gold three-pointed crown. Her raised left hand holds the shining monstrance around which a corner of her cloak is wrapped; her right hand supports the base. The monstrance has golden rays and a silvery center. This, and the presence of what is probably the traditional tower at the left, although it is much obscured in muddy brown color, and the presence of a dark green palm branch in the lower right-hand corner make possible the identification of the figure.

The composition is poor, and the drawing of the figure is awkward. The flesh tones of both the face and the hands are quite well handled. The rather stiff pose suggests that this might have been copied from a richly polychromed statue, although there is no pattern on her garments.

The canvas is severely bruised and damaged. It came from Mexico shortly after 1917 during the political upheavals, along with Nos. 96, 97, 98, and 99. They were presented to Santa Barbara Mission early in 1953 by Mr. Russel Ruiz.

96. ST. BONAVENTURE (?)

This representation of St. Bonaventure is very probably from the same studio as the St. Barbara, Figure 134. The canvas is so badly damaged, and the pigments so bruised and rubbed off that in some sections the background is virtually obliterated.

The Saint stands in the traditional pose, with a cloth-covered table at the left on which are two blue glass inkstands and the open book. The table is out of drawing, for the objects lie behind rather than before him. He wears a very dark brown habit and a lighter brown cape over it. The fact that he wears a beard casts some doubt on this being St. Bonaventure, although the face is fairly young and the head is tonsured. The color and the painting of the hands and head is very good; remarkably distinct are the sensitively drawn slender hands, quite incongruous with the rest of the work.

The painting was given to the Mission by Mr. Russel Ruiz early in 1953.

Cat. No. 96—
Fig. 135.   ST. BONAVENTURE.
Oil on canvas.   22x30.

97. ST. FILOMENA (?)

This full-length figure of a matronly woman saint is an oil on canvas very much like the St. Bonaventure of Figure 135. She stands with her upturned face about to move to the left, with her hands folded before her on her breast; in the crook of her left arm is a single staff of a lily plant, which has three beautifully painted open lilies and one bud at its tip. The lilies are similar to those usually associated with paintings of St. Joseph.

Cat. No. 97—
Fig. 136. ST. FILOMENA.
Oil on canvas. 22x30.

She is dressed in a very full blue gown with a golden brown robe over it. Her full veil is grey-blue. She is standing on a terrace or balcony in front of a brown balustrade, beyond which is a mass of trees. To the right and above her is a theatrically massed drapery or curtain painted in red and red-orange. There is a broken column or pillar in the left foreground. The colors are very yellowed from old varnishes, virtually obscuring the blues of the sky background.

This is quite possibly a representation of the Roman St. Filomena, whose remains were discovered early in the nineteenth century in the Catacomb of Priscilla in Rome. The remains were presumed to be those of an early Christian martyr (about 303 A.D.). Following the discovery, several visions by priests established the claims of the Saint, and the relics were enclosed in a case made in the form of a human body. Many miracles were performed and her shrine, at Mugnano, became very popular.

The painting was presented to Santa Barbara Mission by Mr. Russel Ruiz early in 1953.

98. ST. OMABUONO (?)

This impressive work is a figure of an elderly man clothed in long blue tunic trimmed at the throat and wrists with white ruching, over which is a bright red-orange robe not unlike the robe of the early university doctors. The head is excellently painted; the flesh tones are lifelike and the head is well modeled. The upturned eyes are blue, and there is a thin circlet of a halo over the balding head. His robe is trimmed with an edging of grey fur, and his feet are shod in shoes or slippers. Like the St. Filomena of Figure 136, he stands on a terrace or balcony, but he is facing to the right. The two paintings may well have been companion pieces on either side of a larger central work. The same balustrade and landscape with trees and clouds make up the background.

This is quite possibly a representation of St. Omabuono, a citizen of Cremona, who, though not a religious, was admitted to the canon of the Saints for his great piety and charity. Not only did he feed and care for the poor, but he encouraged repentance and virtuous living. He is generally represented, as he is here, in a fur-trimmed robe worn over a loose tunic. While he is usually pictured in the act of distributing alms, and with a wine flask near, these symbols are not present in this painting.

Figures 135, 136, and 137 were undoubtedly painted in the same studio, if not from the hand of the same artist; the treatment of the delicate, slender hands attests to their common origin. The faces in each have considerable character, and the entire drawing is similar. The characteristic aristocratic hand, with the long delicate fingers, is one of the features of the work of the Flemish artist Van Dyck, whose portraits of the aristocracy very probably found their way to Mexico through engravings and became the prototypes for certain religious as well as secular paintings. Though in all three works the faces are especially sensitive and painted with a degree of characterization that is not too common in lesser painters, the remaining parts of the compositions are much more conventionally realized.

The painting was presented to Mission Santa Barbara by Mr. Russel Ruiz early in 1953.

Cat. No. 98—
Fig. 137. ST. OMABUONO.
Oil on canvas. 22x30.

Cat. No. 99—
Fig. 138. THE DIVINE SHEPERDESS.
Oil on canvas. 20x30.

99. THE DIVINE SHEPHERDESS

Unquestionably this rather charming work is of the late eighteenth century; it is a sincere but quite primitive copy of either a superior painting, or a composite of several, to which additions by the present painter were made.

Our Lady sits under a large tree; around her are several sheep whose eyes are more like those of humans than of sheep. The drawing, especially of the heads, is somewhat conventionalized and stiff. They are white and grey. She is patting the head of one with her extended right hand; in the other she holds a pink and red rose. Her gown is a very bright red; the overdress is of white, tied at the waist with a precise blue bow-knotted belt, and over the waist is another very fine blue ribbon and bow. Her full cloak is blue.

The tree behind her is badly painted and now a muddy brown color. Throughout the tree and over the shrubs behind her are miraculously growing roses of white, pink, and red, and a scattering of other similarly colored "flowers," mere dabs of paint. There is a remarkably straight and unusual shepherd's crook painted across the crook of her arm, a long thin shaft of what appears to be iron; the crook has a right angle and looks more like half of a trident than a crook. Its pointed end makes it appear to be an instrument for prodding rather than for hooking.

The face of Our Lady has an affected, somewhat Victorian charm with its pink and white skin, red-orange lips, and soft brown hair. The face remotely resembles that of St. Joseph in Figure 76; it looks as though it were an adaptation with the figure reversed. Further comparison suggests that this may be from the same studio (of Ayala), with the gaudy flowers a later addition, for there is considerable similarity in such details as the tied bows, the folds of the drapery, and the painting of the eyes.

However, the general pose and attitude of the figure indicate that it was freely adapted from a celebrated painting of *La Divina Pastora* by the Mexican painter Páez. His is a much more elaborate work, with more lambs, small children, two angels floating above the Virgin about to place an ornate crown on her head, and, in the distance, St. Michael freeing a sheep from the clutches of a wild beast. In comparison with the Páez, the Santa Barbara work is crude and primitive.[19]

This painting was presented to the Mission by Mr. Russel Ruiz early in 1953.

100. The Old Reredos *Lienzo:* St. Joachim

Historically speaking, this painting of St. Joachim and its companion piece, St. Anne, are perhaps the most important in the Mission. Together with the remaining fragments of the once large reredos painting, they constitute the largest mural work on canvas in any of the missions. The *lienzo* (linen or burlap canvas) painting dates probably from the dedication of the church in 1825, or possibly a few years earlier. After the church was severely damaged in the 1925 earthquake, a new Reredos was designed and built, and the huge painting —actually a group of paintings—was dismantled and stored away.

The figure of St. Joachim occupied only a small portion of the whole work, the upper left corner. Probably to emulate the elaborately carved and decorated churches of Mexico, and lacking both the artists and the means to duplicate them, the local padres resorted to the next best device: that of imitation. By means of fairly skillful painting of columns, arches, finials, and other architectural devices, and by simulat-

Cat. No. 100—Fig. 139. ST. JOACHIM.
Oil on canvas. Fragment.

ing colored stone work, and by painting statues set in niches, a considerable degree of elaborateness was achieved.

This large mural, with its combination of painted figures and frames or panels for real sculpture, was approximately 26 feet across, or wide, and very nearly the same height. It was horizontally and vertically pieced, the horizontal strips varying from 30 to 37 inches in width. They are now so frayed that an accurate measurement is not feasible. Reference to Figure 23 will show how the work looked before it was dismantled. The lower center section is obscured by the altar, and unfortunately both it and the center section of the upper tier are missing. The heavy garland of flowers near the ceiling was not a part of this painting, but as was the case at San Miguel and at Santa Ines, was painted directly on the wooden or plaster wall back of the high altar.

It is interesting to speculate on just why this elaborate painting was put on canvas to be affixed to the wall, instead of painting it directly on the Reredos. It is also quite possible, although there are no records to substantiate this supposition, that the actual painting may have been done elsewhere to specifications and then brought to Santa Barbara and fastened to the wall. Furthermore, in spite of the strikingly different total effect, the detail work in several portions is markedly similar to the painting of the walls at San Miguel. The architectural details, however, more closely resemble the Reredos at Santa Ines. The entire work may have been planned by one person, but it was obviously drawn and painted by several, each with a different approach and facility. There is marked difference in the techniques of the faces, the figures, the architectural details, and the larger flat areas.

The figure of St. Joachim is very simply and broadly executed; there is a minimum of detail, and only in the carefully executed bow-tie of the waist cord or belt does one see a personal and naive touch. It is all done with flat, simple brush work that appears to be a combination of oil color and of distemper. The head of Joachim is excellently done and very likely is a copy of some now unknown painting, in sharp contrast to the stiffly set body. He wears a long dark robe over which he has a cloak with slit sleeves. It is painted a dark red and is lined with fur. He is painted as though he were a statue in a niche, that like all the other "niches," was painted a light blue. The cove with its fluted or grooved-domed ceiling, somewhat like the inside of a pecten shell, was painted with yellow and grey stripes radiating outward. Proceeding from the niche to the pilasters that enframe it on each side, there is a succession of architectural motifs alternating with plain surfaces that creates a markedly effective sense of form. The motifs and devices were logically derived from the Vitruvius text in the Mission library. The colors used were a dull red, then a "chain" pattern now a gilt color outlined in black, then an area of dark grey. Above each niche in the top tier was a quite realistically painted garland of roses. Directly above and in the center, and hence almost at the very top of the mural, was a winged angel head, rather flat and decorative in its treatment and decidedly Mexican in style.

On the extreme sides, to the left of St. Joachim, and (on the opposite side of the mural) to the extreme right of St. Anne, the enclosing flat pilaster was topped by an urn-like finial, a characteristic neo-classic motif here very simply painted.

Above the niche and to the right of it (hence toward the center of the Reredos) are two seated angels outlined against the blue background representing the sky behind this architectural fantasy. In this respect a Spanish-Colonial tradition was retained: that of more or less repeating in the Reredos the architectural character of the entrance to the church. However, there is absolutely no relationship between the façade of the Mission church and the Reredos. These angels, or *putti,* especially one figure, are derived from late seventeenth-century Italian models. There is a remarkably fine decorative quality in the lines of these small *putti,* but the faulty and awkward drawing of the faces has somewhat spoiled the desired effect.

Cat. No. 101—Fig. 140. ST. ANNE.
Oil on canvas. Fragment.

101. The Old Reredos *Lienzo:* St. Anne

As the counterpart of the St. Joachim, the painting of St. Anne occupies the upper right corner panel of the Reredos mural. The figure is enclosed in a niche exactly like that of its counterpart, but the painting of the Saint is more compact in its outline, and like the St. Joachim, faces toward the center. There is some modeling in the features, which are well realized and obviously the work of a professional decorator. She wears a light grey veil over her enveloping dark grey-brown cloak. The colors, which are laid down quite flat, are those which are repeated throughout the large work: warm brown, dull blue, light blue, yellow, greys, dark red, and black.

102. The Old Reredos *Lienzo:* Panel Background

Of the remaining areas on the Reredos mural, several were niches left blank in the center with decorated borders. The large center area of the upper tier, which had a more complex design than did those on the sides and below, served as a background for the statue of St. Barbara. It has not been found. But from Figure 23 it is possible to assume that its inner area color was a darker blue than that of the others, while on each side was a narrow panel strikingly like those in Roman and Pompeiian villas: decorated with urns holding flowers and ornamental devices.

Figure 141 is part of the panel. It is from the lower right corner, which served as a background for the statue of St. Joseph. On the opposite side of the Reredos was its counterpart for the statue of the Immaculate Conception. Like the backgrounds for the painted statues of St. Anne and St. Joachim, the center space is simply and flatly painted a light blue with decorative borders. The dark outline of the statue of St. Joseph can clearly be seen for in that area the color has not faded. These lower panels were framed on the outside with egg-and-dart and plain borders, then by flat "marble" pilasters topped by Ionic volutes having flower garlands suspended from them. On the innerside, toward the center of the Reredos, there are two of these pilasters. These were whitish shafts with highly colored capitals that combined the Ionic volute with acanthus leaves. Bright colors: red, yellow, and blue were used, not unlike the boldness of ancient Egyptian decoration. The effect of these must have been very striking.

In spite of the fact that his whole Reredos painting—considering all the units or fragments as one whole—was to represent an elaborate architectural Reredos, there was relatively little attempt made to create a sense of three-dimensional form as was the case both at San Miguel and Santa Ines. There is very little shading on the pilasters, the molding, or the arched portions. The result, save for the striking contrasts of the dark figures against the light backgrounds, was strongly decorative and quite flat. In that respect it must have been more arresting in its effect than the far more elaborate work at the other missions, where simulated devices were used.

Cat. No. 102—
Fig. 141. PANEL BACKGROUND.
Oil on canvas. Fragment.

The blank areas here in the center of the upper tier and in the lower one afforded space where (as at Santa Ines) paintings could be hung, or against which statues could be placed. The statues were set on brackets or pedestals either affixed to the Reredos wall by cutting through the *lienzo,* or built up from the floor.

There are now only five pieces of the large work remaining: the two containing the figures, the two lower side panels, and a fragment of what was the center section of the lower tier. The *lienzo* was partly repainted at some undetermined time with ordinary oil paint. Most of the pigment in the older, unretouched areas is extremely dry and brittle, and because the sections have been tightly folded and rolled for storage, the pigment is cracked and falling away from the ground. The backs of these canvases have also been painted in oil colors, presumably to protect them from dampness. They are in very poor condition and within a few years will lose all the surface pigment.

103. MUSIC MANUSCRIPT

The California padres laid considerable stress on music in their instruction of the Indian neophytes, and much was written and copied to help not only with the teaching, but for the performances. Every mission had a wide assortment of hand-lettered music ranging from beautiful, elaborately illuminated choir books and missals on parchment of considerable size, to small works such as this example.

The work here illustrated is an unbound manuscript of fourteen pages of fine quality paper. The paper has fine laid lines and bears two watermarks. One is a large medallion having the letters "H C" or "H G" joined and surmounted by an eagle with outspread wings standing on a globe. On another part of the sheet is a second watermark that can be read as an "L" or a "J" depending on the way it is held. The watermarks are fine lined and lighter than the ground.

The manuscript was made by pasting two of these fine sheets back to back so as to make a less transparent page. They were sewn together about one-eighth of an inch from the left edge with heavy linen thread. The pages are numbered from 1 to 14, with the first page containing the heading and the last or back, left blank. The title or cover page is inscribed in dark brown ink, by Pacífico Capena, as a "Misa a Cataluna," the "first of December, 1842." On the following pages is the music itself.

There are four staffs to each page; each staff is made up of six ruled lines which are not all evenly spaced, and drawn with brown ink. This use of the six-line staff in place of the more modern five-line staff is a reversion to very early (pre-Gregorian) musical notation, and, in the light of the recent date, is inexplicable. The music was written for three voices, with the notation in the Gregorian manner. It appears to be in the key of D-minor. The top notes, or, more correctly, Gregorian notations, are yellow with dark outlines, the middle notes (for the middle voice) are in red, and the lower ones are in grey-black.

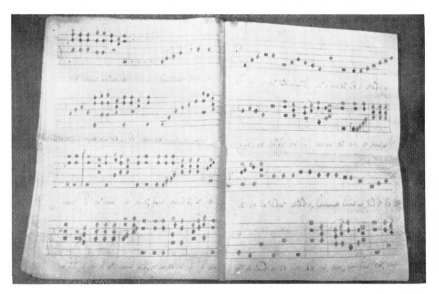

Cat. No. 103—Fig. 142. MUSIC MANUSCRIPT. Ink on paper. 12x16.

The notes are square, rectangular, and diamond-shaped.[20] The signature is made up of three elongated diamond shapes, and there is a sharp sign in the third space. There is also an occasional trill sign used.

The text is in Latin, hand lettered in a rather cursive print, in brown ink below each staff.

S-104. CHASUBLE

Each mission in California has a collection of church vestments, some of which are of considerable antiquity. Within the limits of this work it is possible to note only one example, an old chasuble.

Cat. No. S-104—Fig. 143. CHASUBLE. Damask.

This vestment is made from a beautiful piece of damask that is probably Chinese in origin. It has an intricate pattern of green, silver, and gold leaves and stems, with red and white flowers that appear to be peonies and daisies. Some of the leaves are woven with silver threads. Light and dark blue ribbons are used to tie the stems into bunches. The total effect of these colors and the subtle gradation of light and dark on a milky ground results in an extremely rich effect.

The chasuble has been patched and sewn together in several places and, from its general appearance, must have seen much use.

S-105. MONSTRANCE

Although this small monstrance is not a particularly fine example of the metal work that was produced for the Church in Mexico, it is representative of the general style. It is made of silver-plated brass.

Cat. No. S-105—Fig. 144.   MONSTRANCE.
Silver-plated brass. 17x7.

Most of the silver coating has worn off, and the piece is rather dull looking. The workmanship of the parts is quite ordinary and the designs not too carefully executed. In the decorative design of the grapevine, for instance, the leaves and the grapes are rough and reveal hasty incision or carving, indicating a commercial rather than an artistic approach. The designs and the motifs used are traditional, but not executed with finesse or imagination.

The Luna is of heavy glass approximately 2⅜ inches in diameter, and has a gold-plated inner edge lining. It is surrounded by a design of clouds in high relief that was separately made and attached to the rays spreading out from the center.

This monstrance was probably used on a side altar. It is unquestionably of Mexican origin and dates probably from the early nineteenth century or even later.

S-106. BURSE

The burse or bursary is a part of the vestment set, being placed on the chalice at the beginning and end of the Holy Sacrifice. The burse generally is decorated and in the same colors as are the other vestments. This is an excellent example of nineteenth-century relief and chenille embroidery on a base of heavy silk.

The design on the front is primarily a leaf and flower pattern encircling the Cross and a figure of the Immaculate Conception. These designs have been appliquéd in chenille of different shades of green and blue-green. Here and there in the pattern of the leaves are clusters of what appear to be grapes; these are clear blue jewels (probably very good blue glass). These likewise were appliquéd. The cross itself, which with the Conception dominates the central area, was richly embroidered not only with green threads, but with small, crudely cut gold beads. In the center of the cross is a small blue gem surrounded by four Mexican fire opals about 3/16 of an inch in diameter. Each is encircled with small gold beads. Above the cross, also in beads, are three small opals, probably signifying the Holy Trinity.

At the base of the cross stands the Conception or the Woman of the Apocalypse. The figure is in high relief, made partly of cloth, over which the now faded blue and white garments were sculpturally and very realistically modeled and sewn. The head was a flat piece of soft wood on which was pasted a colored lithographed picture of the Virgin. The hands were similarly pasted on. From the palms of her hands issue rays of golden beads. Below her, enclosed in an oval medallion, is the writhing serpent of evil. It had originally been richly embroidered in color.

The back of the burse has an altogether different pattern. It is covered with three main designs. Again enframing the two center subjects is the vine in green, with tendrils and clusters of grapes, which are here made of bright red glass. Silghtly above center is a cross created with chenille embroidery, in the center of which is a piece of clear cut glass. At the four ends of the cross are oval areas of red silk. The base is entwined with garlands in greens, yellows, and red. Below this are two entwined hearts. They are thickly embroidered in red chenille with intertwining gold and red beads. The one on the right has a sword made of gold beads piercing it.

Cat. No. S-106—
Fig. 145. BURSE (Front).
Embroidery on silk. 9x11.

Cat. No. S-106—
Fig. 146. BURSE (Back).
Embroidery on silk.

The burse has seen much use and is very much tattered and damaged. The design is probably based on earlier motifs. The use of chenille in embroidery probably originated in Europe, where chenille was first used as a cheap substitute for expensive wools and silks in the manufacture of rugs. The thread is considered a novelty yarn and from time to time is used in embroidery. Its first use dates from about 1839 when it was developed in Scotland. Its employment for rugs spread rapidly and became common for trimming during the later years of the nineteenth century. The characteristic fuzziness of chenille yarn gives to the work, especially to embroidery, a softness of edge not otherwise achieved.

S-107. COPPER CENSER

At first glance this copper piece appears to be a locally made pitcher. However, inside is a paper on which the following printed excerpt from a printed catalog is pasted. It reads:

> . . .: Antique Copper Censer. Height 10 inches. Made by the Franciscans who came with Columbus and afterwards went to Mexico with Cortez. After the loss of their sacred vessels by the attacks of the Indians "(see Bernal Diaz)" [*sic*] they supplied the loss by converting their copper cooking utensils into the necessary service for the celebration of Mass.
>
> The above was purchased in 1878 from the Marquis de Mota, a descendant of the Gutierrez family, who lived in Mexico from 1550 to 1558.
>
> Probably the earliest specimen of this work manufactured in America.

On the back of this slip of paper is written: "From Mrs. Augustus Tower, c/o Central Union Trust Co., N. Y. C."

This pitcher, or more correctly, censer, is hand-beaten and riveted copper, made in several sections. The bottom is a molded piece extending about two-thirds of the way up the form from the bottom. There is a heavy seam between the bowl and the neck. The handle was fashioned of two parts mortised together to form the curve; the upper part is split where it reaches the neck, and the two parts are wrapped around at the top of the neck and riveted to it. The two parts join in the front. The lid of the pitcher is attached to the handle with a short heavy brass chain made of three large links.

The workmanship of the piece is similar to the hand hammered copperware produced at many of the missions in the early years of the nineteenth century. To this day similar pieces are being made in the small villages in the mountains of Mexico. In the hamlet of Santa Clara near Patzcuaro, a quite primitive forge is used, and the products made have exactly the same character as this little pitcher-censer.

Barely visible on the side near the bottom of the bowl part is an inscription that was scratched with a sharp tool. The letters are uneven in height and thickness. They are enclosed in a loosely inscribed circle, and may possibly be of later date than the vessel itself. The inscription reads:

    T [?] NE MEQUI
    AFUGIE [or L] TREBO [?] I [or L, T]
    MEI N SANCTI
    O FI CI

Roughly translated, the inscription reads: "Hold or keep me who finds me for my holy office." The inscription seems to substantiate the note found inside the pitcher.

Cat. No. S-107—
Fig. 147. COPPER CENSER.
Hand hammered copper. 9x3.

Cat. No. S-108—
Fig. 148. INDIAN PICTURE FRAME.
Colored wood. 18x22x7.

S-108. INDIAN PICTURE FRAME

This picture frame, though of very little artistic merit, is of historical importance; without doubt it is the work of an Indian neophyte. It is the frame for the missing Face of Christ, also an Indian neophyte work in oil on canvas.

The frame is made of pine covered with thin plaster over which glue was spread. While this was still moist, sand and finely cut gravel or stone were sprinkled. An effective border of dark red triangles was painted over this sand; the pigment used was very likely powdered cinnabar mixed with a binder. On the outer edge of the frame is a double border of small grey-white olivella shells, very carefully placed and set into the plaster or gesso. A few of these are missing.

The frame dates from about 1820 or thereabouts, when the Indian neophytes had achieved considerable dexterity in painting and craftsmanship.

S-109. THE "MOORISH" FOUNTAIN

The so-called Moorish fountain in front of the Mission has been one of the major attractions to visitors for over a century. The fountain was constructed in 1808. Water for it came by way of an aqueduct several miles long, from the canyon to the north. It emptied into the *lavandería* a few yards away.

The fountain proper is set in a wide octagonal basin that has been considerably remodeled since 1808, and which now is a fish pond. It is composed of three principal parts, the bottom of which is a shaft that at one time had carefully cut projecting Ionic volutes of whitish stone. There were apparently four of these, but only one remains in good condition. Resting on this shaft base is the large lower stone basin, some three feet in diameter. The surface is decorated with relief carvings: eight large oval medallions above which is a double row of wavy lines different in detail, and above them a row of radiating, shell-like forms.

The topmost basin is considerably smaller and has for ornament a series of grooves or channels radiating upward from the base. Above this are two successively smaller cylindrical shapes from the topmost of which issues the spray of water.

The carving was undoubtedly the work of the Indians. They had brought with them to the Mission a heritage of stone carving, for their tools and implements had from time immemorial been of stone. Though the fountain has weathered very badly, and some parts of the design have disintegrated due to weathering, the fountain is one monument to the craftsmanship of the Indians. It is rather unfortunate that the Indians were not permitted to make use of their own native design motifs. The fountain, though very much simplified, does not make use of any ornamental devices that were used by them in their own stonework. The design of the fountain is based on the *mudéjar* type introduced into Spain by the Moors, and the types and forms of which were inevitably transported to the New World and as far as Santa Barbara and Carmel.

S-110. BEAR'S HEAD WATERSPOUT

Like the work on the fountain, the *lavandería,* or wash basin, was an object not only of admiration but of wonder to the early visitors to the Mission. The principal object of interest is the stone bear's head which served as a waterspout.

Cat. No. S-109—Fig. 149. THE "MOORISH" FOUNTAIN. Carved sandstone. 8'.

Cat. No. S-110—Fig. 150. BEAR'S HEAD WATERSPOUT.
Carved sandstone. 36".

The head of this spout, with its open mouth through which the water spurted, was carved from native sandstone. It is so badly cracked and weathered that it is impossible to tell whether it was carved from one or from several pieces. Only a vestige of its original outline remains. Still clearly visible are the curious circle-like eyes and the remains of the snout. Only slight humps on the head remain of the ears. The forms of the legs and haunches can scarcely be distinguished. It appears to have been covered with plaster at one time.

The forward part of the beast rests on a pier of adobe fired bricks that were covered with mortar or plaster. The wall behind the spout is also of brick and plaster.

This bear's head is one of the few pieces of Indian sculpture remaining *in situ* in the state of California. It dates from 1808, the year the *lavandería* and the fountain were completed. It is not used at present; in former times the overflow water from the fountain issued from the creature's mouth to fill the large basin below.

S-111. THE CEMETERY DOOR

The door leading from the church to the cemetery is in all older churches commonly decorated with the symbol of death: the skull and crossbones. In those churches the graveyard was generally just outside and adjacent to the sanctuary area of the church. More modern churches no longer have the graveyard, since the cemeteries are as a rule a considerably distance away.

The decoration of the wall immediately above the door facing the burial ground is very striking and dramatic in its simplicity. Directly above the keystone of the arch and immediately below the sill of the window is a skull and crossbones rather crudely cut from native stone. Only the upper portion of the face is carved, the lower jaw having been omitted. This is unquestionably primitive carving and was probably made by the same carver or carvers who made the fountain and the bear's head in the *lavandería*. But far more interesting is the fact that below this stone carving and to each side are two human skulls and thigh bones imbedded in the masonry, but projecting in high relief as does the stone work above them. Parts of the bones have long since disintegrated.

The actual doorway is framed in a simple Roman-type arch that springs from equally simple pillars made of superimposed blocks of stone. Save for an extremely simple incised crisscrossed line on what can pass for the base of the supporting pillar, there is no ornament. The window above the doorway is a splayed opening, with a very simple but beautiful Moorish-style arch at the top. The glass window itself, which is set in the thickness of the wall, is rectangular and smaller in dimensions than the outer shape.

Cat. No. S-111—Fig. 151.   CEMETERY DOOR DECORATIONS

Notes

Notes

NOTES TO THE INTRODUCTION

Frontispiece. According to story, the original of this oil painting of Father Junípero Serra hung for many years in the Franciscan Convent of the Holy Cross in Querétaro, Mexico. From there it was moved to the Convent of Santa Clara, and finally in 1900, it was transferred to the Franciscan Convent of St. Francis, both of which were also in Querétaro. At the beginning of the Mexican Revolution, around 1910, the original painting was destroyed, or at any rate, it disappeared. Señor Salvador Herrera, of Querétaro, attested to these facts in a letter to Fr. Zephyrin Engelhardt, O.F.M., in October, 1924. His brother confirmed at Querétaro in 1945 that he, too, had seen the original painting at Querétaro before 1910. However, investigations made recently by Fr. Maynard Geiger, O.F.M., offer no proof that such an original ever existed at Querétaro.

Purported copies in oil of the "original" were claimed to have been made at Querétaro by a priest named J. Mosqueda, now deceased. One of these copies hangs in the sacristy of the Holy Cross Convent in Querétaro. The other copy is at the Old Mission in Santa Barbara (the original of the photograph). They are identical down to the finest details, although the Santa Barbara copy is somewhat larger. The size is 19¾ by 25½ inches.

Junípero Serra was born November 24, 1713, at the Villa de Petra on the island of Mallorca off the coast of Spain. He joined the Franciscan Order at the age of sixteen, and subsequently became not only a brilliant student, but a professor of theology and philosophy.

In the world, Serra became a conqueror. Though outwardly mild and humble, a fire of devoted enthusiasm raged within him. He was an issue of the conquistadors, he waging war on paganism, they battling armed Indians, and while he secured for Christ, they gained for Charles. In 1749 he volunteered for missionary service in Mexico, and thereafter followed a lifetime of labor and sacrifice for the Church. Five months after his arrival in Mexico City in 1750 he was sent to the fierce and unfriendly Indians in the isolated Sierra Gorda district northeast of Querétaro. He worked eight years on this mission and brought to the Indians not only civilization but the life of the Faith. For the next seven years he traveled extensively in Mexico, always preaching and spreading the Faith.

When Padre Serra was fifty-six years old, he began the great work of founding the California missions. In founding the first nine of the twenty-one he confirmed almost 6,000 Indian converts. Not only this, but from his labors grew the great coastal cities of California. The foundation of the present agricultural system in the state was laid by him, for his labor was a combination of the spiritual and the physical for the welfare of his converts. Serra died at Carmel Mission (San Carlos Borromeo) on August 28, 1784.

[1] *The Architecture of the Missions,* in Annual Publications of the Historical Society of Southern California, Los Angeles, Calif., 1907-1908 (Vol. VII).

[2] H. H. Bancroft, *History of California. [Bancroft's Works,* Vols. 18-24.] (San Francisco: The History Co., 1882-1891), *passim.*

[3] Fray Juan de Torquemada, O.F.M., wrote a three-volume work on New Spain entitled *Monarchia Indiana,* published at Madrid in 1613 and at Seville in 1615. A later edition was published in 1723 by N. Rodríguez Franco at Madrid.

[4] M. G. Holway, *Art of the Old World in New Spain* (San Francisco: A. M. Robertson, 1922), pp. 26-28.

[5] Stirling-Maxwell, *Annals of the Artists of Spain* (London: John C. Nimmo, 1891), Vol. 1.

[6] Werner Weissbach, in his *Spanish Baroque Art* (Cambridge University Press, 1941), gives an excellent and authoritative summary of the arts of this period.

[7] *Twenty Centuries of Mexican Art* [Catalog of an Exhibition] With an introduction by Antonio Leal. (New York: Museum of Modern Art, 1940), p. 69.

[8] H. H. Bancroft, *California Pastorale. [Bancroft's Works,* Vol. 34.] (San Francisco: The History Co., 1898), pp. 103-104.

[9] J. F. G. de La Pérouse, *Voyage,* etc. (Paris: Imprimerie de la République, 1797), Vol. II. An illuminating commentary on La Pérouse is found in the second volume of Engelhardt's *Missions and Missionaries of California* (2nd ed.; Santa Barbara: Mission Santa Barbara, 1930), pp. 698-701.

[10] Engelhardt, *op. cit.,* pp. 114-115. He is quoting from Palóu's *Vida,* Cap. xxix, 130. There is in the possession of the Southwest Museum of Los Angeles a painting which is purported to be the original picture mentioned in the statement by Palóu. However, the painting is not a banner, though it might well have been mounted on stretchers at a later date. It is undoubtedly an old work and of fair merit; it is damaged and almost entirely covered with cracks. The accompanying illustrations (Figures 2 and 3), especially Figure 2, are in no sense accurate representations of the scene, for not only are the Indians incorrectly dressed, but the two priests are vested in garments for the celebration of the Mass, and the picture depicted on the banner is also imaginary. It is quite probable that the original painting of the account mentioned had been removed from its stretcher for easier transportation, and that one of the padres simply unrolled the canvas in the presence of the natives.

Although there is no positive proof of the identity of this canvas in the Southwest Museum, the name is the same. Tradition has it that it hung in San Gabriel Mission before the secularization and disappeared from there when the missions were secularized. It was subsequently restored to the Mission by Father Juan Caballería, who re-collected many of the dispersed mission paintings. The collection, of which the picture in question is a part, was purchased from him by public subscription and is now in the Casa de Adobe of the Southwest Museum. See also *Outwest Magazine* (Los Angeles), September, 1904 (Vol. xxi, No. 3), pp. 210-230.

Mission San Buenaventura has several canvas "banners" hung from standards in its collection; for better preservation any of these could be mounted on stretchers and framed.

[11] Quoted by Engelhardt, *Santa Barbara Mission* (San Francisco: The James H. Barry Co., 1923), p. 151.

[12] J. M. Letts, *California Illustrated* (New York: Holdredge, 1853), p. 137.

[13] An instance of this can be found in this excerpt from a letter written by Fray Francisco Palóu to Fray Juan Sancho (the Guardian of San Fernando College) in Mexico City, from Mission San Carlos on September 13, 1784: "Since God willed that the death of my beloved father should be in your Reverence's triennium, if you wish to order it [a portrait of Father Serra] painted, I should be very much pleased, and in case someone is inspired and there is a benefactor, we will accept it for Masses or for the stipends which we will all take kindly. The most edifying scene would be to have him wearing his stole and kneeling before the altar of Our Lady, with the Child in her arms, and a priest vested with a cope before the altar, with a small host for giving him the viaticum, and coming from the lips of the dead father in verse *Tantum Ergo,* with many Indians and leather-jackets with their candles in their hands. In case you think well of it I will write by the land post, suggesting the title that might be put beneath it. . . ." (Translated into English from the manuscript in the Archives of Mexico, and edited by H. E. Bolton, in his *Historical Memoirs of New California by Fray Francisco Palóu* [Berkeley: University of California Press, 1926], iv, 365.)

On the following February 6, 1785, Fr. Sancho wrote from Mexico the following: "The picture of the deceased Fray Junípero is being painted at the expense of his Reverence, Bishop Verger . . ." (*ibid.,* p. 376).

There is evidence regarding the outcome of this request, for the painting, formerly in San Fernando Convent, now hangs in the Room of the Missionaries in Chapultepec Castle, Mexico City. It is a large canvas about six feet long, and in fair condition. It is signed: "Marriannus Guerrero Fecit a 1785." This brief exchange of letters, of which the quoted material is but a small part, is among the only documentary evidence concerning paintings; unfortunately nothing pertaining to the works in the missions has yet been found. The original documents are in the Museo Nacional de Mexico. (Documentes Relativos a las Misiones de California, MS [Quarto Series], Vol. III.)

[14] The Pious Fund, begun in 1697 in Mexico, was the aggregate of sums that had been donated by Spanish and Mexican Catholics for the establishment of missions in the two Californias. Some assistance had been given toward the missions, but this money did not come from the government. During the first years of his reign, Philip V donated an annual pension of 13,000 pesos, and the Viceroy had personally lent some assistance in the

founding of the first missions in Baja California. By 1735 the Jesuits received large donations to be used for the propagation of the Faith. They administered the funds so well, through investments, that the income therefrom not only supported the wants of their missions, but added to the capital. The accumulations of the Fund in 1767, when the Jesuits were expelled from Mexico, included great tracts of land, mines, flocks, estates, as well as cash.

It cost some 10,000 pesos (now about $1,000.00) to establish and maintain a mission. Upon the removal of the Jesuits, the government "administered" the assets of the Pious Fund. From that time on it provided only 1,000 pesos (or Mexican dollars) for the complete establishment of a mission. Eventually the entire fund was confiscated by the Mexican government. Though the California missions were entrusted to the Apostolic College of San Fernando, they depended largely on the Fund for support. Following the Hidalgo Revolt in 1810, the stipends derived therefrom ceased for some time. In 1827 the Mexican government confiscated about 78,000 pesos on deposit; in 1832 the Congress passed a decree that diverted the entire fund into the National Treasury. Although subsequent decrees (as in 1836) provided some financial support for the missions, the amounts received were pitifully inadequate. The government spent little if anything on the missions. The rights of the Church to sums due it from the Pious Fund were the subject of extensive litigation after 1846.

Although the principal financial support of the missions was the Pious Fund, there were three other means of "support." An initial grant (*ayudas de costa*) of the equivalent of $1,000.00 was made to pay for equipment. The annual stipends (*sínodos*) were usually paid by the government and varied according to the remoteness of the mission. For California it was about $450.00. Included in the "support" was the military protection, inasmuch as the royal treasury paid the wages of the guards and, for a time at least, gave them financial aid. See Herbert Bolton, "The Mission as a Frontier Institution," *American Historical Review,* XXIII (1917), pp. 42-61; William Gleeson, *History of the Catholic Church in California* (San Francisco: A. L. Bancroft & Co., 1871-1882); Engelhardt, *Missions and Missionaries,* Vols. II and III; G. W. James, *In and Out of the Old Missions* (Boston: Little, Brown & Co., 1907), especially chapter xxxiv.

[15] The full text of the secularization decree of May 1, 1834, and subsequent legislation is given by Engelhardt on pp. 515-532 in his *Missions and Missionaries,* etc., Vol. III. Subsequent chapters are a history of the decline of the mission system.

NOTES TO OLD MISSION AT SANTA BARBARA

[1] The three padres were "three barefooted Carmelites, namely Father Andrés de la Asumpción, or Asunción, Father Antonio de la Ascensión, and Father Tomás de Aquino . . ." (*The Voyage of Sebastián Vizcaíno,* quoted in Engelhardt, *Mission Santa Barbara,* p. 17).

[2] Engelhardt, *op. cit.,* p. 52.

[3] *Ibid.,* pp. 53-54.

[4] *Ibid.,* p. 63. The Immaculate Conception generally represents the Virgin Mary standing on the crescent moon; the statue of this description now on the Reredos lacks the crescent. A faded blueprint photograph taken between 1874 and 1883 (Figure 13) shows an Immaculate Conception back of the altar. The crescent was probably lost during the restoration of 1926. There were also two statues of St. Joseph in polychromed wood. Engelhardt says that the two figures were "six palms in height and they were placed on the two altars which stood against the side walls of the sanctuary painted this year (1795)". The St. Joseph mentioned is the smaller one now on the Reredos, the other is now at Mission San Antonio.

[5] There is however, no mention of "large" oil paintings in the inventories of that year. The inventories of 1797 listed the Stations of the Cross. It is quite possible that the paintings referred to are either the Coronation of the Virgin and the Crucifixion, or the lunettes of Our Lady of Mount Carmel, and the Last Judgment, (both of which are now on loan to Mission San Antonio de Padua). These four were the only really large paintings in the Mission.

[6] James, *In and Out of the Missions* (p. 360 and plate 44c), refers to the piece as the "Archangel Miguel."

[7] Engelhardt, *op. cit.,* p. 86.

[8] *Ibid., pp.* 90-91, quoting the report of December 31, 1812, by Fathers Gil and Amestoy.

[9] *Ibid.,* pp. 101-102, gives interesting evidence.

[10] *Ibid.,* p. 111, citing the annual Mission report.

[11] Duhaut-Cilly, quoted in Engelhardt, *op. cit.,* pp. 150-154.

[12] Discovery by Father Maynard Geiger, O.F.M., historian at the Old Mission. See the *Santa Barbara News Press* for February 18, 1951. During the reconstruction of 1952, Father Thaddeus Kreye, O.F.M., architectural adviser to the Restoration Project, made additional discoveries relative to the successive stages in the development of the present buildings. His findings are summarized in an article written for the *Santa Barbara News Press* of November 16, 1952. Marie T. Walsh in her *Mission Bells of California* incorrectly quotes Robinson as saying that there were two towers at the date of his first (1829) visit to California. There is no mention of the towers in the account of his visit of 1829-1830 in the *Life in California* editions of 1846 or 1891.

[13] Alfred Robinson, *Life in California* (San Francisco: William Doxey, 1891), p. 44. See also pp. 276-278. There were several editions of this work. The first was published in 1846 by Wiley and Putnam in New York. Issued and bound with this was Fr. Gerónimo Boscana's *Chinigchinich.* The 1851 edition was published in London by Collins, and it appeared without the Boscana Work. The 1891 edition (San Francisco: Doxey), also omitted the Boscana but contained an appendix. A reprint of the first edition was edited and published by Thomas C. Russell in San Francisco in 1925.

Another appeared in 1947, edited by Joseph A. Sullivan. It contains colored lithographs and was published by Bio Books at Oakland, California.

[14] Robinson, *op cit.,* 1891 edition, p. 56. See also Figure 4.

[15] John Bodkin, *Santa Barbara Mission* (Los Angeles: Privately printed, 1910).

[16] Quoted by Engelhardt, *op. cit.,* p. 113. The sculptures are fully described in the catalogue. The reconstructed ceiling designs can be seen in the Mission church; the canvas pieces *(lienzos)* with the paintings of the saints were recently rediscovered and listed in the catalogue: Figures 139, 140, 141.

[17] Engelhardt, *op. cit.,* pp. 152-154.

[18] Fr. Thaddeus Kreye, O.F.M., of Mission Santa Barbara, who is preparing a definitive history of the architecture of Mission Santa Barbara, concurs in this opinion. The Alden watercolor painting (Figure 78) shows some kind of balcony just under the eaves. If the chronology of Mission construction is correct, then the Alden painting must be of early date, for it clearly indicates a *roofed over* balcony, and one with a very high parapet. Though the drawing of many of these artists is not always to be trusted, here is clear evidence of a structural detail that was never mentioned as such in the chronicles. Alden may have exaggerated the height of the parapet or railing.

[19] Brewer, *Up and Down California* (New Haven, 1930), pp. 56-57.

[20] J. J. O'Keefe, *Buildings and Churches of the Mission* (Santa Barbara, 1886).

[21] (Mrs.) Ayda Addis Storke, *A Memorial and Biographical History . . . of Santa Barbara . . .* (Chicago, 1891), p. 76.

[22] The present chapel is dedicated to St. Anthony.

[23] A type of side altar, as in Figure 14. The custom of erecting and dedicating side altars may change with each pastor. The painting remains on the wall of the Mission church, but there is now no altar. From this description one would judge the church to have been rather cluttered. The photograph has the positions of the altars and the paintings exactly reversed.

[24] These are Numbers 92 and 93 in the catalogue. Both paintings were sent on loan to Mission San Antonio de Padua at Jolon in 1950.

[25] This now hangs in the Sacristy.

[26] John Bodkin, *op. cit., passim.*

[27] A reprint of a very interesting news item dated Nov. 25, 1879, appeared in *The Santa Barbara News-Press* for Nov. 25, 1954: "The Mission Church is undergoing extensive repairs, including a new ceiling, the old one being somewhat dilapidated. Mr. Tom Martin has in his possession two wrought-iron nails taken from the ceiling of the Mission Church a few days ago, which look as bright and new as though they had just been forged. They have been in the building for over 90 years." Quite obviously the unknown writer of the news item was in error, for the church building did not date back to before 1820.

[28] See note 24, above.

[29] James, *op. cit.,* p. 330.

[30] *Ibid.*, pp. 331-332.

[31] See also Edith Webb, *Indian Life at the Old Missions.* Her chapter 17, "Indian Artists," is the only comprehensive and documented study of the talents and techniques of the California Indians that has been published.

[32] Mary G. Holway, *Art of the Old World in New Spain* (San Francisco, 1922), pp. 133-135. This author is not clear as to the source of some of her data, especially with reference to the originals of some of the paintings, nor is there accurate identification of several of the figures. Although this is perhaps the first book dealing with the art objects in the California missions, material is far too sketchy to be of much value. Furthermore, the term *chancel* is not commonly used in the Roman Catholic Church; the area to which Holway refers is the sanctuary.

[33] This is now the chapel dedicated to St. Anthony.

[34] The saints are Michael, Raphael, and Gabriel.

[35] Catalogue No. 32. The saints are either St. Agnes of Assisi or St. Agnes of Prague, St. Clare, and St. Margaret of Cortona, not the Virgin Mother, nor the penitent Magdalen. The painting is described in the catalogue.

[36] For a detailed description of the earthquake and the damage, and of the subsequent reconstruction, see M. T. Walsh, *The Mission Bells of California* (San Francisco, 1934), and Hildegard Hawthorne, *California Missions* (New York, 1942).

NOTES TO THE CATALOGUE

[*] This catalogue by no means lists all the art and craft objects in the Mission "collection," many of which pieces are of more than passing interest. There are a number of pieces of wood sculpture, carvings, etc., of the modern period, or imitations of earlier works, and many paintings and prints which have been omitted. There are, for example, seventeen paintings in oil by John Sykes of different missions; only the one of Santa Barbara has been listed. The vestment collection is represented by one piece, as are the several fine examples of missals, choir books, and other early printed or hand lettered books. There are some good examples of hand worked copper, of leather work, and of wood carving, the latter very probably Indian work. There are also several pieces of eighteenth-century silver. In the old kitchen of the museum room, in addition to the partial restoration of the ovens, can be found numerous examples of Indian stone work: mortars, pestles, *manos,* and *metates;* elsewhere there are the memorabilia of the nineteenth-century clergy: the crucifixes, rosaries, boxes, and other personal belongings and souvenirs of great interest, but having no place in this catalogue.

[1] Excellent analyses and photographs of Baroque sculpture are to be found in Pál Kelemen, *Baroque and Rococo in Latin America* (New York: Macmillan Co., 1951), the outstanding work of its kind, and in Diego Angulo Iñiguez, *Historia del Arte Hispanoamericano* (2 vols.; Barcelona and Mexico: Salvat Editores, S. A., 1945, 1950), especially Vol. II, and in Manuel Toussaint, *Arte Colonial en México* (Mexico: Imprenta Universitaria, 1948).

[2] For a complete history of the Franciscan habit and the numerous minor variations, see Raphael Huber, *Documented History of the Franciscan Order* (Milwaukee: Nowiny, 1944), pp. 669-688.

[3] Engelhardt, *Mission Santa Inés* (Santa Barbara: Mission Santa Barbara, 1932), pp. 54-56, and *passim*.

[4] Numerous writers have, without foundation, stated that this painting was the work of Murillo.

Bartolomé Esteban Murillo was born December 31, 1617, in Seville and died there in 1682. Without question, his influence on the subsequent painting of Spain and hence of the New World was greater than that of any of the Italians. As the popular religious painter of Spain, he ranks second only to the Italian masters. That his work had influence on the Mexican painters of the seventeenth and eighteenth centuries is obvious in the many Murillo-derived paintings seen in the churches and cathedrals there, for even his very early works, rough and crude as they were, were purchased for the colonies. At Seville he worked for three years for the Franciscan convent near the Casa del Arjumentamiento, where he began the large canvases with life-sized figures; it was during this time that he developed his particular naturalism and individual style.

By 1670 Murillo had reached the height of his fame. Painting as he did for the conventual churches, hospitals, and sacristies, he had for the most part to represent the subjects that pleased the devout of the day: the Immaculate Conceptions, the visions in monks' cells, the mysteries and ecstasies of the religious. Of most significance are the paintings executed during the period of his peculiar style known as *el vaporoso,* since it had a misty or vaporous effect. Spain of the seventeenth century was not only intensely religious but also pervaded with a sentimental devotion to religion. All religious works were painted along a prescribed plan, an emotional type of religious art mainly characteristic of Andalusia, and since Murillo's plans were ready-made, his procedures were simple. He was a mannered painter; his color is ordinarily unctuous and consistent rather than vigorous.

Stories that Murillo made a visit to America are to be found in many biographies derived from Sandrart and others. These stories may have been founded on the fact that of his two sons, the elder, Gabriel Esteban Murillo, went to America. There are a number of Murillos in Mexican churches, and presumably might be in California. The influence of the Murillo school on Colonial painting was felt directly. Whether it was inspired by the Murillo canvases sent to the West Indies and to Mexico, or by the work of Gabriel Murillo (who was reputedly painting in the West Indies), there was a rather remarkable change in the color of the painting, from a relatively somber quality in the seventeenth century, to a more luminous, brilliant scheme in the eighteenth century.

Murillo's imitators were numerous even during his lifetime, for his style and coloring was easily imitated. The one thing, however, that his imitators generally failed in was the drawing, for none of them succeeded in reaching his level of painting the soft, supple forms, nor the charming humanity and personality of his characters. His best "follower" was Cabrera.

Miguel Cabrera was believed to have been a Zapotec Indian born in Oaxaca in 1695. He died in 1768. He was a painter and engraver and a master of excellent composition. He was especially noted for the beauty of his female heads and faces. The coloring of his figures was fresh and soft, bearing the traits of Murillo. He was at times called the Mexican Michelangelo, at others, the Murillo of Mexico. He maintained a very large studio where copies of old masters were frequently made. He had many assistants of considerable ability and turned out a prodigious number of works, some of tremendous size. Although he ranked high among his contemporaries, becoming the first director of the Academy of Fine Arts in Mexico City, he has been criticized for being too "pretty" and thus having hastened the decadence of painting in Mexico.

[5] Though the Zacatecan Franciscans did not enter into California missionary work until late in the mission period, it is significant that so many mission paintings resemble the Zacatecan style originals more than they do those at San Fernando. It is not unlikely that a considerable and very active school of painting existed at Zacatecas, and it is quite possible that works were contracted for even from as far as San Fernando in Mexico City. They may have been gifts to the padres, although the mention of the value of the Stations suggests that they were purchased. The other great Franciscan center, Santa Cruz at Querétaro, was, with San Miguel de Allende, a center for wood carving and sculpture, especially in the late seventeenth and the eighteenth centuries.

[6] Nicolás Juárez, or Xuárez, was born in Mexico in 1667 and died in 1734, a prominent member of a large family of important painters. His brother Juan Rodríguez was considered the most able of the group. The work of Nicolás was of sufficient merit to warrant comparison with that of the great Spanish master Zurbarán. His work was characterized by fluent technique, careful attention to the expressions of his subjects, and a certain nostalgia of the spirit. He was a considerable influence on Mexican painting, considered by some writers as forming the starting point for Ibarra, Cabrera, and others.

Among the painters influenced by Juárez was Miguel de Herrera (not the Friar of the same name), a fairly competent but uneven artist active during the middle of the eighteenth century. Although his figure works, especially the "portraits," are distinguished by a certain characterization, there is a tendency toward softness and the sentimental. A St. Joseph and Christ Child by him dated 1778 is in the Lamborn Collection of the Philadelphia Museum of Art. The Santa Barbara canvas, if it is from his studio, is superior in every way. (See also Note 10, below.)

[7] José de Ibarra, a native of Guadalajara, was born in 1688. He has often been compared with both Correggio and Murillo, and became, with Cabrera, the chief exponent of Murillo in the New World. His works are characterized by the extensive use of reds and blues, and a certain theatrical mannerism that was in the tradition of the Baroque. He followed fully, and with great

success, the improvements introduced in Mexican painting by the Juárez brothers. He achieved great fame during his life time. He died in Mexico in 1756.

[8] The original for this work may have come from Querétaro, for in the Franciscan convent church at El Pueblito nearby, there is almost the identical painting. The drawing, and what remains of the painting, are very good and in the tradition and style of the late seventeenth century. If this is the original Carmel painting, then it can be considered one of the first brought to California.

Subjects of this character were common in Colonial Mexico; there is an excellent example of such a group realized in sculpture, on a small side altar in the Church of Santa Cruz in Querétaro.

[9] Although St. Rose of Lima was a Third Order Dominican, because of her saintliness and good work in the New World, she was very frequently painted in company with Franciscans. Paintings of her are found in many Franciscan churches, especially in South America. Murillo's painting of her became the prototype of many Spanish-colonial works and unquestionably, in a more remote manner, the source for the figure of St. Agnes of Assisi represented in this painting.

[10] This rather spectacular painting has in it the characteristics of two Mexican works, first the color, and to some extent, the figure of the Christ of the Crucifixion by Miguel Herrera in the "museum" at Guadalupe-Zacatecas; secondly, the more dramatic quality, though none of the movement, of Sebastián de Arteaga's Christ on the Cross in the Mexico City cathedral. Herrera was active during the last half of the eighteenth century, principally in and around Mexico City. The dates of his birth and death are not known. Though a fairly fluent draftsman, the color of the majority of his works is rather dry and cold. (Cf. Chavez, *Tres Siglos de Pintura,* etc., p. 307.) Arteaga was born in Seville and came to Mexico in 1633, carrying with him to Mexico some of the more austere qualities of Spanish art, qualities which were manifested in his later painting. He was an officer of the Inquisition in Mexico and painted the portraits of his associates. Although a very capable painter, his style as well as the quality of his work varied considerably. Nevertheless, he ranked as an important painter of the mid-seventeenth century (Cf. Chavez, *op. cit.,* plates 28-31 and pp. 203, 204.)

It is quite possible that the painter of the Santa Barbara Crucifixion might has drawn from both works for inspiration.

[11] A mural painting of this same subject is in the Franciscan cathedral founded in 1529 at Cuernevaca, Mexico. There is a very fine canvas of the Apocalypse at Mission San Luis Rey, but it is much more Flemish (Rubens-like) in character, than it is Mexican. The Mission Inn at Riverside, California, has an oil painting almost identical in composition with the Santa Barbara version. In it the stars about the Virgin's head are clearly in evidence, but the St. Michael is in the act of slaying the dragon, and the upper portion of the canvas seems to have been cut off, for the figure of God the Father, though present, is not as complete. The entire coloring is also somewhat

lighter. In some respects the technical aspects of this painting are superior to the Santa Barbara canvas. It is also much smaller, being only about 18 by 24 inches, and according to records at the Inn, was presumed to have been painted about 1700 in Mexico. Although very badly damaged, with much pigment worn off, the Santa Barbara work is a superior painting, for it has the warmth and richness of color that was so typical of the later Murillo influence on Mexican painting, especially from the studios of Juárez, Ibarra, and Cabrera. Unquestionably the three paintings under discussion were derived from the very large and magnificent canvas by Cabrera in the former convent of Guadalupe-Zacatecas. That canvas, however, had been severly mutilated, for the entire central section had at one time been cut out of the picture. It was "restored" several years ago.

[12] In the "museum" at Guadalupe-Zacatecas (Mexico), there is a good portrait in oils of Bishop García y Diego; it is, however, rectangular, and the head is turned slightly to the side. It is an extraordinarily sensitive work. There is no signature; the painting is probably the work of one of the resident friars, several of whom are known to have been excellent painters. The physical resemblance of the Santa Barbara work and the painting at Zacatecas point to the same origin, although the location of the original of the photograph is not known.

[13] Engelhardt, *Santa Barbara Mission,* p. 62.

[14] The *Refugio* (Our Lady of Refuge) by José Alzibar, a popular eighteenth-century Mexican painter, was obviously the prototype for this work. Alzibar's painting has, however, far more elaborate detail in the garments; there are clusters of roses in the corners, jeweled crowns, and a halo of stars. An almost saccharine sweetness dominates the work. The poses of the two figures in the respective paintings are nearly identical, only in the suppression of detail for the general improvement of the Santa Barbara canvas, do the paintings differ. Alzibar was born about 1727 and died in the early years of the nineteenth century. He was a prolific painter and one of the founders of the Academy of Painters established in 1753 in Mexico City. His Virgins, Holy Children, Angels, and other figures, have a distinctive personal style, amiable and elegant and the compositions of his works are varied and rich with ornament. His paintings are in many Mexican churches and museums. (Cf. Chavez, *op cit.,* plates 97, 98, and pp. 285-287.)

[15] Details of this little statuette can be compared with a statue, *Nuestra Señora del Pueblito,* made by Fr. Sebastián Gallegos, a Franciscan of the Province of San Pedro y San Pablo, and an engraving dated 1776 indicated as being a "faithful portrait of that Miraculous Image." The engraving is reproduced on the cover of *El Palacio* (December, 1949, no. 12). The similarity in details of the Santa Barbara statue and the engraving, especially of the ornaments of the gown, is striking, and even the archcrown is similar. The engraving, however, does not show the Virgin with the Child, who is shown in the lower right-hand corner; furthermore, St. Francis is also present, holding up the three globes. It is quite possible that the engraver took liberties when he derived from the original figure, such as the position of the hands, and in the omission of the Infant. The Santa Barbara figure may

conceivably be a contemporary copy of the Gallegos statue, if not from his studio, but the general crudity of the work indicates that it is in no sense the product of a skilled wood carver. The original statue is in the Franciscan convent church at Pueblito, near Querétaro.

[16] There are several versions of this painting in the California Missions. The one at Mission Santa Ines is almost identical in size, pose, drawing, and the crude coloring, but it has the striking addition of the severed head of the vanquished Maximin beneath the point of the sword. The fact that the two paintings are so similar points to the quantity production of religious art of dubious aesthetic merit in the latter years of the Mission period. Yet this canvas is a valuable index to the history of taste and standards in religious art of the late Spanish-Mexican period.

[17] The drawing of this Altar immediately calls to mind the sanctuary—and especially the Reredos—of Mission Santa Ines. Remarkably similar are the "marbleized" patterns, the garlands, and the painted niche above the tabernacle. It may be mere coincidence that this similarity exists, but since the Santa Ines decorations were completed probably in 1825, it is not inconceivable that the same artist may have had a hand in the work. A close comparison will reveal even further similarities, especially in the matter of details: the shading, the motifs, and very probably the coloring. This is quite logical, since Bishop Diego was active around Santa Ines, where the first California college (or seminary) was founded by him.

[18] There is a similar painting at Mission San Luis Rey, but rectangular in shape and somewhat larger. It contains many more figures. Careful comparison of the two works reveals that the San Luis Rey painting is superior in many respects, and that it is more complete in its details and the complement of figures. The Santa Barbara work, aside from its different shape, appears to be a simplified copy. The general areas (save for the upper corners) are alike; the Christ is identical, as are the more important lesser figures. The medallions to the side, however, are dissimilar in both shape and the representation of the subjects.

The San Luis Rey work was brought to the Mission from Zacatecas. It very probably dates from the early eighteenth century, to judge from the complex composition and the strong Baroque character of many of the figures. The Santa Barbara painting is probably a slightly later copy, or, more correctly, a version.

[19] A print of the Páez work can be found in Francisco Dies Barroso's *El Arte en Nueva España* (Mexico, n. p., 1921), figure 231. Mission Santa Ines has a large and tapestry-like *Divina Pastora,* signed "de la Mora." Although it likewise is an adaptation of the Páez work, and though it is far superior to the Santa Barbara version in many respects, it is a minor painting. The facial characteristics suggest that the date is also somewhat later, probably early nineteenth century. The history of the devotion and portrayal of this subject—which rarely appears outside of Spanish and Spanish-Colonial Art —is interestingly related by Marie T. Walsh in her *Mission of the Passes,* (Los Angeles: The Times-Mirror Press, 1930), p. 63.

[20] The most comprehensive and informative work on the music of the California missions is by Owen da Silva, O. F. M., *Mission Music of California* (Los Angeles: Warren Lewis, 1941).

Chronology of Acquisitions

Dates followed by an asterisk (*) refer to first mention in Mission Inventories

There are no acquisition dates for the following pieces:

Cat. No.

S-8	High Altar Crucifix
S-9	Old Sanctuary Lamp
38	Mission San Carlos Borromeo
44	The Virgin of the Apocalypse
46	St. Joseph and the Christ Child
47	Bishop García Diego
49	Painting of the Mission by Dieppa
S-52	St. Anthony
S-55	Crucifix
S-59	Classical Tabernacle
62	The Holy Trinity
S-63	Woman Saint or Angel
S-65	Standing Figure
66	Painting of the Mission and Seminary
69	St. Michael and the Holy Trinity
71	St. Anthony and the Christ Child
77	"Mexican" Madonna and Child
85	Mission Santa Barbara in 1890
S-88	The Crucifixion Group
S-103	Music Manuscript
S-104	Vestments
S-105	Monstrance
S-106	Burse or Bursary
S-107	Copper Censer
S-108	Indian Picture Frame

Glossary

ADOBE

The name given to a rather heavy, clayey, sticky soil; specifically, a large brick made principally of clayey soil and mixed with straw, formed and sun-dried; it also signifies a building constructed of this material.

ALTAR CARDS

Generally, a set of three printed, painted, or manuscript cards put upright on the altar to assist the memory of the celebrant. They are removed and laid flat when Mass is not being said.

ALTAR PIECE

A painting at the back of an altar, either by itself or as part of the reredos (*q.v.*); generally a painted or frescoed picture on the wall above the altar.

ALTAR SCREEN

Originally, a piece of ornamental precious cloth hung above the altar at the rear. Later a permanent (or movable) structure of wood, stone, or metal was used. The side facing the church is called the retable.

AUREOLE

In Roman Catholic theology, a celestial crown added to the bliss of heaven for those who have triumphed with signal success in their conflict with the world, as for virgins, martyrs, doctors, or preachers. In early times it was used only in representations of God. In art, it is the indication of a glory or halo around the head or whole body of a sacred personage. It is often indicated by a narrow circle at a distance from the head (a halo), in relief sculpture by a gilded ring maintained by slight supports. When the aureole is of pointed oval shape, of two arcs of circles surrounding the entire personage, it is called a *vesica piscis*.

DIADEM

Ribbons or bands of linen or silk (sometimes of thin gold) worn around the head and passing over the temples. In a crown, it refers to the arch over the head.

GLORY

An emanation of light proceeding from a being of peculiar sanctity. Commonly represented by rays of gold, a golden circle, or disc around the head or body. The glory is the general term for the aureole and nimbus.

HALO

Commonly, a circle or arc of light surrounding the head of Christ or of a saint. It symbolizes holiness, the light of grace.

PREDELLA

The step, or ledge, on the rear edge of the altar on which stand the decorations, Crucifix, and candlesticks. Also called the *gradine*. Also, the paintings or other decorations on the front or riser of the ledge. Sometimes (incorrectly) the entire altarpiece with the altar step on which it stands.

MONSTRANCE

Another name for the Ostensorium, *q.v.*

NIMBUS

A circle, disc, or any indication of radiant light around the head of divinities, saints, and sovereigns. The nimbus is, technically, a luminous vapor or atmosphere surrounding a person. The common form for Christ is circular with three arms of the Cross within it; for a saint it is a circle with rays enclosed. The Greek form for God the Father was triangular. The square nimbus was used on representations of living persons. In early Christian art, it was used arbitrarily as an emblem of human greatness, not only divinity.

OSTENSORIUM

The monstrance. Originally, any receptacle in which sacred relics were exposed to view; now a decorated metal vessel, gold or silver plated, with a transparent section in which the Sacred Host is carried in processions or exposed for adoration. Also, an emblem in art associated with St. Clare of Assisi, whose proper attribute it is, alluding to an incident whereby, in holding aloft the Monstrance, she miraculously dispersed the Saracens.

POLYCHROMY

The term applied to the process of decoration, especially sculpture and architecture, in which several colors are used, applied over a gesso ground.

POLYCHROMED (WOOD)

Sculpture that has been colored, generally after receiving a coating of linen, gesso, or plaster, over which other colors are applied.

REREDOS

A carved, or otherwise ornamented screen of wood or stone at the back of an altar; a painting in the same position; a combination of the two. It may be separate or structurally a part of the altar. Sometimes it is the back wall of the Church behind the altar (as in Santa Barbara and San Juan Capistrano.)

RETABLE

Generally, the face or covering of the altar screen, raised above the rear of the altar to support lights, ornaments, etc. It is usually decorated with painted scenes, or in relief. When this retable or altar screen is ornamented with painted panels and enriched with

niches and statues, and often painted in brilliant colors, it is called a reredos. Sometimes this reredos extends across the whole breadth of the Church and up to the ceiling.

SACRED HEART

A devotion to Jesus Christ, consisting in the divine worship of His heart of flesh considered as united to His divinity, and as the symbol of His love for man. It is essentially the worship of Jesus Himself. This devotion is a modern version of the ancient conception of Jesus as the Good Shepherd and dates from about 1675, when it was first publicly preached.

SCAPULAR

Two small pieces of wool cloth, about two by three inches, joined by strings and worn under the clothes. They are badges worn with confidence in the mercy and might of God. The brown scapular is the badge of the Confraternity of Our Lady of Mt. Carmel. There is also a scapular medal which under certain conditions takes the place of the other, bearing an image of Our Lady on one side, and of the Sacred Heart on the other.

SANCTUARY

The most sacred part of the Church, reserved for the place of the high altar and the clergy; in older churches it was in the apse, but now, more generally, it means the area separated from the nave by the communion railing.

SACRISTY

A room or apartment adjoining the church in which the vestments, books, and sacred vessels are kept and where the clergy vest for their office.

STATIONS OF THE CROSS

A series of fourteen paintings (sometimes relief sculpture) depicting the events of the journey of Christ on the road to Calvary, His Crucifixion, and Entombment. It remains a devotion introduced by St. Francis and popularized in its present form by St. Leonard of Port Maurice as a symbolic presentation of the Way of the Cross. It is especially important in Church devotions during Holy Week.

TABERNACLE

The cupboard-like receptacle on the altar, wherein is reserved the Blessed Sacrament. It is universally used in the Latin rite. It is made of wood, stone, or metal, and the top is preferably domed or pyramidal. The interior is lined with silk. The doors are often decorated either with symbols or paintings.

Bibliography

BANCROFT, HUBERT HOWE. *California Pastoral.* (Historical Works, Vol. 34.) San Francisco: The History Co., 1898.

BARROSO, FRANCISCO DIES. *El Arte en Nueva España.* Mexico, 1921.

BEATTIE, GEORGE WILLIAM. *California's Unbuilt Missions.* Privately printed, 1930.

BERGER, JOHN A. *The Franciscan Mission of California.* New York: Doubleday, 1948.

BLACKMAR, FRANK W. *Spanish Institutions of the Southwest.* Baltimore: Johns Hopkins Press, 1891.

BODKIN, JOHN. *Santa Barbara Mission.* Los Angeles: Bodkin, 1903.

BOLTON, HERBERT E. (ed.). *Anza's California Expeditions,* Vol. I. Berkeley: University of California Press, 1930.

————. (ed.). *Font's Complete Diary.* Berkeley: University of California Press, 1933.

————. "The Missions as a Frontier Institution . . .," *American Historical Review,* XXIII (October, 1917), 42-61.

BOYD, E. "A New Mexican Retablo," *El Palacio* (Santa Fe, N.M.), 56, no. 12 (December, 1949), 355-7.

BREWER, WILLIAM H. *Up and Down California in 1860-1864,* ed. FRANCIS P. FARQUAR. New Haven: Yale University Press, 1930.

CARTER, CHARLES F. *Missions of Nueva California.* San Francisco: Whitaker and Ray, 1900.

CAUGHEY, JOHN W. *California.* New York: Prentice-Hall, 1940.

CHAPMAN, CHARLES E. *A History of California: The Spanish Period.* New York: Macmillan, 1930.

CHASE, J. SMEATON, and SAUNDERS, C. F. *The California Padres and Their Missions.* Boston: Houghton Mifflin, 1915.

CHÁVEZ, AUGUSTIN VELÁSQUEZ. *Tres Siglos de Pintura Colonial Mexicana.* Mexico: Editorial Polis, 1939.

CLINCH, BRYAN J. *California and Its Missions.* 2 vols. San Francisco: Whitaker, 1904.

COY, OWEN C. *Pictorial History of California.* Berkeley: University of California Press, 1925.

CURTIS, CHARLES B. *Velasquez and Murillo: A Descriptive and Historical Catalogue.* New York: Bonton, 1883.

DE MOFRAS, DUFLOT. *Travels on the Pacific Coast.* 2 vols. Translated, edited, and annotated by EYER WILBUR. Santa Ana: Fine Arts Press, 1937.

DAVIS, N. *The Old Missions of California.* Oakland: Claremont Press, 1926.

DOYLE, J. T. "The Missions of Alta California," *Century Magazine,* Vol. XLI, new series, Vol. XIX (1890-91), pp. 389-402.

ELDER, PAUL. *The Old Spanish Missions of California.* San Francisco: Elder, 1913.

ENGELHARDT, ZEPHYRIN. *Missions and Missionaries of California.* 4 vols. 2nd ed. Santa Barbara: Mission Santa Barbara, 1930.

————. *Santa Barbara Mission.* San Francisco: Barry, 1923.

FORBES, MRS. ARMITAGE S.C. (Harriet Rebecca Piper). *California Missions and Landmarks.* 8th ed. Los Angeles: Privately printed, 1925.

GEIGER, MAYNARD. *Calendar of Documents in the Santa Barbara Mission Archives.* Washington, D.C.: Academy of American Franciscan History, 1947.

GLEESON, W. *History of the Catholic Church in California.* 2 vols. San Francisco: Bancroft, 1872.

GOLDSMITH, ELIZABETH. *Sacred Symbols in Art.* 2nd ed. New York: G. P. Putnam's Sons, 1911-12.

GUDDE, ERWIN G. *California Place Names.* Berkeley and Los Angeles: University of California Press, 1949.

HALL, TROWBRIDGE. *California Trails.* New York: Macmillan, 1920.

HALLENBECK, CLEVE. *Spanish Missions of the Old Southwest.* New York: Doubleday Page, 1926.

HAWTHORNE, HILDEGARD. *California Missions, Their Romance and Beauty.* New York: Appleton Century, 1942.

HERRERA CARRILLO, PABLO. *Fr. Junípero Serra.* Mexico: Xochitl, 1943.

HOLWAY, MARY GORDON. *Art of the Old World in New Spain and the Mission Days of Alta California.* San Francisco: Robertson, 1922.

HUBER, RAPHAEL M. *Documented History of the Franciscan Order.* Milwaukee: Nowiny, 1944.

HUDSON, WILLIAM HENRY. *The Famous Missions of California.* New York: Dodge, 1901.

JACKSON, HELEN HUNT. *Glimpses of California and the Missions.* Boston: Little, Brown, 1902.

JAMES, GEORGE WHARTON. *Old Missions and Mission Indians of California.* Los Angeles: Baumgardt, 1889.

————. *In and Out of the Missions.* Boston: Little, Brown, 1906, 1907.

————. *The Old Franciscan Missions of California.* new ed. Boston: Little, Brown, 1925.

JUDSON, WILLIAM L. "The Architecture of the Missions," *Annual Publications of the Historical Society of Southern California, 1907-1908.* Vol. VIII, Parts II-III.

KELEMEN, PÁL. *Baroque and Rococo in Latin America.* New York: Macmillan, 1951.

LA PÉROUSE, J. F. G. DE. *Voyage de La Pérouse Autour du Monde.* Redigé par M.L.A. MILET-MUREAU. Tome II. Paris: Imprimerie de la République, 1797.

LETTS, J. M. *California Illustrated.* New York: R. T. Young, 1853.

LEWIS, OSCAR. *California Heritage.* New York: Crowell, 1949.

NEWCOMB, REXFORD. *The Old Mission Churches and Historic Houses of California.* Philadelphia: Lippincott, 1925.

News Notes of California Libraries, V, No. 3 (July, 1910).

O'KEEFE, JOSEPH J. *Buildings and Churches of the Mission of Santa Barbara.* Santa Barbara: Independent Printing House, 1886.

OLDER, MRS. FREMONT. *California Missions and Their Romance.* New York: Coward-McCann, 1938.

PALLEN, C. B. and WYNNE, J. J. (eds.). *New Catholic Dictionary.* New York: Universal Knowledge Foundation, 1949.

PALOU, FRANCISCO. *Historical Memoirs of New California,* ed. HERBERT BOLTON. 5 vols. Berkeley: University of California Press, 1926.

PRIESTLEY, HERBERT I. *Franciscan Explorations in California,* ed. LILLIAN E. FISHER. Glendale, California: Arthur H. Clark, 1946.

RICHMAN, IRVING B. *California Under Spain and Mexico.* Boston: Houghton Mifflin, 1911.

ROBINSON, ALFRED. *Life in California.* New York: Wiley and Putnam, 1846.

SMITH, FRANCES RAND. *Architectural History of Mission San Carlos Borromeo.* Sacramento: California Historical Survey Commission, 1921.

STIRLING-MAXWELL, WILLIAM. *Annals of the Artists of Spain,* Vol. I. London: Nimmo, 1891.

STORKE, YDA ADDIS. *A Memorial and Biographical History of Santa Barbara . . . and Ventura Counties.* Chicago: Lewis, 1891.

TORCHIANA, H. A. VAN C. *Story of the Mission Santa Cruz.* San Francisco: Elder, 1933.

VANCOUVER, GEORGE. *A Voyage of Discovery to the North Pacific Ocean.* . . .
3 vols. London: Robinson, 1798.

VILLA AGUSTIN F. *Antigua Escuela de Pintura en México,* ed. ALFONSO TORO.
2nd ed. Mexico: Quijote, 1919.

VIZCAINO, SEBASTIÁN. *The Voyage of.* . . . San Francisco: The Book Club,
1933.

VISCHER, EDUARD. *Missions of Upper California.* San Francisco: Winterburn,
1872.

WALSH, MARIE T. *The Missions Bells of California.* San Francisco: Wagner,
1934.

WEBB, EDITH BUCKLAND. *Indian Life at the Old Missions.* Los Angeles:
Lewis, 1952.

WEISSBACH, WERNER. *Spanish Baroque Art.* Cambridge: Cambridge University Press, 1941.

Index